DAILY EXPRESS

HOW TO CUT YOUR TAX BILL

Without Breaking the Law

Grant Thornton

1996/97 EDITION

GW00707841

KOGAN
PAGE

YOURS TO HAVE AND TO HOLD

BUT NOT TO COPY

The publication you are reading is protected by copyright law. This means that the publisher could take you and your employer to court and claim heavy legal damages if you make unauthorised photocopies from these pages. Photocopying copyright material without permission is no different from stealing a magazine from a newsagent, only it doesn't seem like theft.

The Copyright Licensing Agency (CLA) is an organisation which issues licences to bring photocopying within the law. It has designed licensing services to cover all kinds of special needs in business, education and government.

If you take photocopies from books, magazines and periodicals at work your employer should be licensed with CLA. Make sure you are protected by a photocopying licence.

The Copyright Licensing Agency Limited, 90 Tottenham Court Road, London, W1P 0LP. Tel: 0171 436 5931. Fax: 0171 436 3986.

First published in 1994
Second edition 1995
Third edition 1996

Apart from any fair dealing for the purposes of research or private study, or criticism or review, as permitted under the Copyright, Designs and Patents Act, 1988, this publication may only be reproduced, stored or transmitted, in any form or by any means, with the prior permission in writing of the publishers, or in the case of reprographic reproduction in accordance with the terms of licences issued by the CLA. Enquiries concerning reproduction outside those terms should be sent to the publishers at the undermentioned address:

Kogan Page Limited
120 Pentonville Road
London N1 9JN

© Grant Thornton, 1994, 1995, 1996

British Library Cataloguing in Publication Data
A CIP record for this book is available from the British Library.

ISBN 0 7494 2016 2

Typeset by Saxon Graphics Ltd, Derby
Printed in England by Clays Ltd, St Ives plc

Contents

Contributors

PETER ARROWSMITH

RAY ASHURST

STEWART AYLWARD

BRIAN CONNELL

OWEN CONNOLLY

GEOFF EDWARDS

DAVID FULLER

JAMES GIBSON

MICHELE HADDICAN

MICHAEL HOLLIS

NICK KEMP

JOHN LOEBL

DAVID MARGERISON

IAN MILES

JOHN MILLETT

TOM O'CONNELL

DAVID PAYNE

NIGEL POLE

MAUREEN SALE

GLENNIS SMITH

NEIL STURMEY

TINA WINTER

Foreword to the First Edition

Have you ever wondered how you can save on the amount of tax you pay? If so, then this book is for you.

It has been estimated that as many as three-quarters of all taxpayers pay too much tax — either in error, or unnecessarily. The sums involved are incredible — as much as £8 billion has been highlighted and all of it due to a lack of understanding, a lack of planning and a lack of action.*

Tax affects all aspects of our lives. This guide will help you gain a better understanding of how the tax system works. In its pages you can discover the effect that tax and national insurance have on your working life, whether you are employed, working for yourself or retired. By understanding the tax consequences of different types of savings and investment you can make the system work for you and save money while increasing your wealth. You can also refer to helpful chapters on all financial aspects of family life from marriage to death, and from home to life assurance.

Saving tax should not be an end in itself. Action should never be taken simply because it is tax efficient. The action must be of benefit to you and your family. For example there is no point in spending your declining years in self-imposed poverty warmed only by the knowledge that you have avoided inheritance tax by giving everything away!

The book has been written from the point of view of the normal taxpayer, born here and living here full time. Complications, and indeed advantages, can arise in other circumstances. The aim of the book is to provide general guidance to the reader, with the purpose of simplifying some of the many complexities that exist. It is always advisable to seek professional guidance where substantial amounts of money or overseas aspects are involved. No book, however eminent, is ever a substitute for specific, personal advice.

* Source: Mintel for IFA Promotion.

This guide has been written by practising taxation and financial planning specialists in Grant Thornton. Their contributions, and that of Christina Cole, who typed the text, are gratefully acknowledged.

Ian Johnson
Editor

The information for this Tax Guide has been supplied by leading business advisers and chartered accountants Grant Thornton. It has been written on the basis of the law and practice in force at 31 October 1995 and incorporates the Budget proposals of 28 November 1995. Grant Thornton, the UK member firm of Grant Thornton International, is authorised by the Institute of Chartered Accountants in England and Wales to carry on investment business. This information is for guidance only and action should not be taken without obtaining specific advice.

Foreword to the Third Edition

This third edition incorporates a number of amendments to the original text, including a new appendix, to reflect the legal position in Scotland.

A further new appendix summarises the changes occasioned by the forthcoming introduction of the new system of Self-Assessment and the move from the present Preceding Year Basis to the new Current Year Basis of assessment for Schedule D. Each in itself is significant; combined they represent the biggest change to the UK tax system since the introduction of PAYE some 50 years ago. While the main text of the book reflects forthcoming changes as appropriate it was thought helpful to summarise the main features of the new system in one place for easy reference.

Once again, the contribution made by colleagues throughout the firm in preparing this guide is gratefully acknowledged.

Ian Johnson
Editor

No man in this country is under the smallest obligation, moral or other, so to arrange his legal relations to his business or to his property as to enable the Inland Revenue to put the largest possible shovel into his stores. The Inland Revenue is not slow — and quite rightly — to take every advantage which is open to it under the taxing statutes for the purpose of depleting the taxpayer's pocket. And the taxpayer is, in like manner, entitled to be astute to prevent, so far as he honestly can, the depletion of his means by the Revenue.

The Lord President (Clyde)
Ayrshire Pullman Motor Services and
D M Ritchie v The Commissioners of
Inland Revenue (1929)

1

Communications from the Inland Revenue

Taxpayers regularly receive three types of communication from the Inland Revenue. These are notices of coding, tax assessments and tax returns. This chapter removes the mystery surrounding these three items.

Notices of coding

Explanation

Many directors and employees receive their new code number from the tax office on Form P2 before the new tax year begins on 6 April.

The code number is the means by which the Inspector tells an employer how much tax to deduct under the Pay As You Earn (PAYE) system. The employer is only told the final code, not how the figure is made up. If the code is incorrect, too much or too little tax may be deducted.

The tax office starts from the tax allowances that have been claimed previously (see Chapter 4). From the figure of total allowances are deducted other items such as benefits in kind (see Chapter 10), state retirement pension or investment income. The tax office uses the PAYE system to collect all the tax due from the employee. This saves having to make an assessment at the end of the year and allows the taxpayer to pay tax evenly and regularly instead of in a lump sum.

Allowances will usually exceed deductions. This means that there will be some tax-free allowances to set against gross pay or pension. The code number leaves off the final figure and adds one of the following letters to indicate which allowance is included:

L   the basic personal allowance;

H   the basic personal allowance plus the married couple's allowance or the additional personal allowance;

P   the allowance for those aged 65–74;

V   the allowance for those aged 65–74 plus the married couple's allowance for those aged 65–74;

T   in most other cases where L, H, P or V do not apply or:
- where the employer is not to know which allowances are received, or
- where the taxpayer is aged 65+ but does not get the basic allowance, or
- where there is a deduction for car benefit in the code.

Thus a single person with no other sources of income will be entitled to the basic personal allowance of £3765 and the code will be 376L.

The letters at the end of the code number instruct the employer as to what action to take when allowances change in the Budget, so every employee does not need a new coding notice immediately. All those with T codes will receive a revised coding each time allowances change.

There are other codes:

BR   all allowances are used against other income, and tax is therefore to be deducted at the basic rate;

DO   tax to be deducted at the higher rate;

NT   no tax to be deducted, for example because the income is going to be included in the professional accounts of a doctor;

OT   similar to BR but the lower rate of tax is to be applied first, then basic rate and then higher rate.

If the code is **BR**, **DO** or **OT**, the tax office have assumed there is other income against which the allowances are used. If this is wrong the tax office should be told immediately (see Chapter 2).

A code beginning with a **K** means that deductions exceed allowances so there is a negative code. Instead of having tax-free allowances to set against pay, extra income is added to pay. This often happens when there are large car benefits.

To check a notice of coding

Has the tax office given the correct allowances? If these are wrong it might mean that they are waiting for a tax return to be sent in. Use the notes that come with the code to check the current allowances.

Are the deductions correct? Do those other sources of income exist? Compare the deductions with the figures on the last tax return.

If something is wrong contact the tax office promptly. Often a quick telephone call will solve the problem and the coding will be amended immediately.

How does the code work?

By using the code and separate tax tables the employer calculates the tax bill. The tax tables divide the tax-free allowance between the number of paydays in the year. If the tax code and salary remain the same an equivalent amount of tax should be paid on each payday.

What happens if the code changes?

If it goes up it means there are more tax-free allowances so less tax is paid. If there is a big increase there may be a refund but usually there will be a smaller tax bill. On the first payday that the new increased code is used any tax overpaid since the previous 6 April will be refunded.

Similarly, if a code goes down, more tax will be paid. Any underpaid tax may be collected on the first payday from which the lower code is used if the amount is small.

Often the Inspector prefers to spread an underpayment over a complete tax year. Any underpaid tax from earlier in the tax year will be left, to be collected later. This will either be by way of an assessment or through a reduction in the allowances of the next tax year.

Tax assessments

These are sent out when, usually, there is more tax to pay. The system will be made simpler with changes which start in the 1996–97 tax year.

The schedular system

For historical reasons all income is divided into schedules.

Assessments usually cover one schedule so a person with complex tax affairs may receive several assessments, sometimes from different tax offices. Under the new system one office will deal with all your tax affairs.

The principal schedules are:

- **Schedule A.** Income from letting property. The amount assessed is the rent receivable less the expenses payable. (See Chapter 16.)
- **Schedule D.** This is divided into several cases.
  - — **Cases I and II.** Profits from businesses and professions.
  - — **Case III.** Interest not taxed before receipt, for example from the National Savings Bank.
  - — **Cases IV and V.** Income from abroad.
  - — **Case VI.** Any income not assessed elsewhere. A common example is casual fees.
- **Schedule E.** Earnings from employments including benefits in kind and pensions. The schedule is divided into three cases depending on where the income is earned and whether the employee lives outside the UK. (See Chapter 14.)
- **Schedule F.** Company dividends.

Capital gains

Disposals of assets such as shares, or property other than a private home, may give rise to a capital gain if sold for more than the original cost. Where the asset was held at 31 March 1982, its value at that date is substituted if this gives a more favourable result in computing the gain. There is an allowance for inflation known as indexation (see Appendix A) together with an annual exemption, for 1996–97 £6300, but if the proceeds exceed these then the excess is taxed as if it were extra income.

Tax bands

After deducting allowances from total income the tax bill is calculated using three tax bands for 1996–97.

- Lower rate   20 per cent up to £3900.
- Basic rate   25 per cent between £3901 and £25,500.
- Higher rate   40 per cent over £25,500.

How to check an assessment

The assessment shows:

- The income.
- The allowances to set against that income.
- The calculation of the tax due.
- What tax has been paid.
- How and when any further tax is to be paid or what tax is repayable.

Each step must be checked carefully. Mistakes happen and if the assessment is wrong the tax office must be told within 30 days. This is called appealing against the assessment. If too much tax is being charged, the tax office must also be requested to postpone payment of the excess.

The income details should agree with the figures on the tax return. All the allowances being claimed should be given. The tax office ought to have written before the assessment was sent if the income or allowances were to be different.

Sometimes the lower rate band is forgotten. If separate assessments on different sources of income are received some allowances or part of the basic rate band might be missed. Always check and appeal if anything is wrong.

Does the assessment give credit for all the tax that has already been paid? Check. Remember to include tax paid under PAYE, tax deducted from dividends or interest and tax paid separately to the Inland Revenue.

Most tax that remains due will be payable direct to the Collector of Taxes and the assessment will incorporate a payslip. If the extra tax relates to salary or pension the tax office will usually agree to collect it by reducing your allowances over the next complete tax year. Always ask if this is possible.

If tax has been overpaid this will normally be refunded shortly after the assessment has been received.

Tax payments

Tax on investment income which has not had tax deducted at source is due on 1 January in the tax year.

Tax on trading profits is due in two instalments on 1 January and 1 July.

Higher rate tax on investment income that had tax deducted at source and on capital gains is due on 1 December following the tax year.

If extra tax on earnings and pensions is to be paid in a lump sum it is due 14 days after the Collector of Taxes issues a demand. This will not be issued until at least 30 days after the assessment is issued.

Under the new system, for 1996–97 any tax due will be payable by 31 January 1998.

Tax returns

Who gets one?

Tax returns are sent to anyone whose income is likely to change from one year to the next. The following might expect to receive one annually:

- The self-employed.
- Company directors.
- Those earning over £8500 per annum with a company car or other benefits.
- Those employees who claim allowances for expenses in connection with their work.
- Those who receive an annual tax refund.
- Those with investment income.

If a return is not received by someone in one of these groups and/or the individual knows that they should be paying more tax the tax office must be informed. Failure to do so may mean paying interest and penalties as well as the extra tax.

Where an annual return is received by someone who is not in one of these groups then check with the tax office. The return may be issued in error or for reasons which no longer apply. The annual chore of filling in the return may be avoided.

Types of return

There are four main types for individuals:

11P Employees earning over £8500, most company directors and high income pensioners.

P1 Other employees, directors and pensioners.

11 Self-employed and those with investment income.

R40 Annual repayment claimants.

Forms **11P** and **11**, the most detailed ones, are very similar. The **P1** is a simplified version of the **11P** but the **R40** is the easiest to complete. Unfortunately the **R40** is only sent if none of the other returns is needed.

Completing the tax return

Chapter 3 explains what needs to be shown on the return. Chapter 4 gives more information about allowances. The Inland Revenue's own guides, sent with every tax return, give much detailed help. Chapter 2 explains how to get the tax office to help with the return. If an individual's tax affairs are complex they will probably benefit from the help of a suitably qualified accountant.

There are penalties and interest for submitting incorrect or late returns. The normal time limit for the completion of a return is 30 days from the date of issue but this is usually extended to 31 October following the end of the tax year. Under the new system from 1996–97, the time limit will be 30 September if you want the tax office to work out your tax bill, but 31 January if you self assess.

Never sign a return until every entry has been carefully checked. In law an individual is responsible for all the entries even if an accountant or someone else completes it on their behalf.

Always keep a copy of the return to help check any notice of coding or assessment.

Summary

- Check whatever you are sent.
- Appeal against incorrect assessments.
- Pay tax on time.
- Keep a copy of your tax return.

2

Dealing with the Inland Revenue and Social Security

Dealing with either department can be a frustrating experience. Understanding something of the structure of local offices can help reduce problems and waiting time.

Both departments have invested much time and effort in training their staff to be more accessible to their 'customers'.

Each department has a charter setting out what can be expected of them and what they can expect from the citizen. The Taxpayer's Charter and the Contributor's Charter are reproduced as Appendices B and C.

Inland Revenue

Structure

The country is divided into regions; each headed by a regional controller responsible for a number of tax offices and collection offices. The staff in tax offices work out what tax is to be paid. That tax is paid to an accounts office but a local collector becomes involved if the tax is not or cannot be paid on time.

The network of local offices is supported by specialist head office departments. Many of these are now located outside London.

There are many complaints about the lack of liaison between accounts offices, local collectors and tax inspectors. The ongoing merger of inspectors' and collectors' offices should improve liaison.

The officer in charge of these new style offices is assisted by several inspectors and collectors, who in turn are assisted by a number of other staff. Inspectors deal with technical points and matters affecting large amounts of tax. Most people have their tax agreed without an inspector being personally involved.

Which office should be contacted?

The office that sent the communication is the one to which response should be made. The three types of communication and their relevant offices are listed below:

Notices of coding and assessments:	Tax offices
Demand notes and payments:	Accounts office
Time to pay and collection problems:	Local collector

The two accounts offices that receive all tax payments are situated in Shipley, Bradford and Cumbernauld, Glasgow. Tax offices in southern England or Wales tend to have Shipley as their accounts office, while Cumbernauld deals with the remaining offices.

Collectors of taxes are based locally. If there are difficulties over payment then the one closest to home or business should be contacted.

It is more difficult finding out which tax office deals with individuals. For most people it will not be their local office.

Employees and those in receipt of a firm's pension will be dealt with by the tax office dealing with their employer. This used to mean the tax office nearest to the employer's payroll office but increasingly this means dealing with an office far from home.

The self-employed will often have two tax offices to deal with: one dealing with their employees and one dealing with their own tax. Usually the latter is near the business even if the PAYE office is far away.

People with investments who claimed annual repayments using a form **R40** were dealt with by their local office. This work has now been centralised.

Other taxpayers are likely to be dealt with by their local inspector.

Contacting the tax office

Since records were computerised, national insurance numbers have been the key to all records. Each individual also has a tax reference number. All employees or pensioners of one firm have the same reference but the self-employed and others have unique personal references. If possible, quote both national insurance number and tax reference.

The reference consists of two parts. The first three digits identify the office and the rest is the reference within that office.

Telephoning

The best method for dealing with straightforward enquiries is to telephone. Typically the phones are manned from 9am to 4.30pm.

When telephoning have both the national insurance number and reference available. Remember that the tax office must be sure they are not giving confidential information to the wrong person.

Ask for the officer's name. This should be given on request. Make a note of what is discussed and what action is promised. Note the date of the call. This will need to be referred to if the promised action does not happen.

Writing

Complex problems and complaints are best handled in writing. Tax offices deal with tens or even hundreds of thousands of taxpayers so ensure the tax reference and national insurance number are always quoted.

Most letters receive a reply within 28 days. If nothing is heard after this time send a reminder or telephone. After another week, a letter to the officer in charge enclosing a copy of the original letter usually brings an immediate reply.

Visiting

If the tax office is at the other end of the country, visiting can be difficult. To help, a network of Taxpayer Enquiry Centres (TECs) are being set up. Telephone any office for the address of the nearest TEC.

The TECs are manned by specially trained staff. They have access via the computer network to all records and can deal with most enquiries without the need to refer to individual files.

Telephone first to check opening times as they vary. Appointments are not usually necessary unless individual files have to be sent from a tax office to the TEC.

When visiting any tax office it is essential to take some form of identification, preferably something showing your national insurance number and tax reference. In collection matters take the assessment or demand note.

The staff at the TEC will explain assessments or notices of coding, how to fill in tax returns or even negotiate time to pay tax.

How to complain

Failure to respond or understand the problem? An unfair or wrong answer? What can be done?

First ask for the matter to be reviewed by the officer in charge. If this does not produce results there are several options for taking the matter further.

Technical points, for example, 'How much of this income is taxable?' or 'Is this deduction allowable?' can be referred to the independent appeal commissioners. These are local people appointed by the Lord Chancellor to hear appeals locally. They listen to both taxpayer and inspector and then make a decision. The hearing is in private.

While the commissioners have the final decision on a point of fact, an appeal can be made to the High Court (the Court of Session in Scotland) if either side believes the commissioners are wrong on a point of law.

More often, complaints involve delays or repeated errors. If the officer in charge cannot help, your next step is to write to the regional controller. Asking the local office for his address will alert them. They might then come up with a solution without actually involving the regional controller.

When taking the complaint further it is helpful to give details of all telephone calls and meetings and enclose copies of correspondence.

Alternatively, the best chance of progressing the matter without involving another Revenue officer might be to enlist the help of the local Member of Parliament (MP). A request from an MP to have a matter reviewed will receive a fast response. Bear in mind that involving an MP will not guarantee success unless the Revenue can be proven wrong.

Perhaps a dozen times a year an MP feels that the matter is insoluble. They will then refer to the Ombudsman. The fullest review will then be undertaken at the highest level.

If an MP is not to be involved and the regional controller has failed to sort out the problem, then the matter can be referred to the Revenue and Contributions Agency Adjudicator who investigates all complaints impartially. Complaints to the Adjudicator must be in writing. Asking for the Adjudicator's address is likely to cause another review of the case.

After the complaint is settled

There is a statutory right to receive interest on delayed refunds. Called repayment supplement, this is paid at a fixed rate, currently 7 per cent, for specified periods.

Although the Revenue used not to pay compensation this is changing. If you employed an accountant to sort out the Revenue's errors, or inconvenience and distress have been suffered, ask for compensation. A reasonable claim supported by details of costs incurred and distress caused should receive sympathetic attention.

If, because of delays in using the information provided, too little tax has been paid and the error subsequently comes to light, some of that extra tax may be waived. This special treatment is called 'official error'.

To qualify for a reduction the individual must have income of less than £40,000, have believed his or her tax affairs to be settled, and have waited at least one complete tax year without being told that extra tax might be due.

The amount to be waived is calculated on a sliding scale depending on income, for example a person whose total income is less than £15,500 would have all the extra tax waived but someone with income of £22,000 would have only half waived. Normally this concession has to be claimed.

How to avoid problems

Many problems are caused by a lack of liaison between the various offices dealing with an individual's tax affairs. Help to prevent this by copying correspondence to each office.

When writing to the inspector saying an assessment is wrong send a copy to the collector to prevent incorrect demands being issued. If two inspectors are dealt with then make sure they both know what is going on.

The Department of Social Security (DSS)
Structure

Local offices are split into two: the Benefits Agency and the Contributions Agency. Their roles are complementary and information supplied to one is usually available to the other.

Each section is headed by a manager, who is ultimately responsible to the agency head. Head office sections, including the refunds section, are based in Newcastle-upon-Tyne.

Which office should be contacted?

This is likely to be the office dealing with an individual's home address. In many telephone directories the entry for Social Security will show which office deals with which postal areas.

An employer should contact the Contributions Agency dealing with the area in which the business is located.

Contacting the DSS

By letter or phone or personal visit. It is important that the national insurance number is given and, for benefit enquiries for an existing claimant, the reference on the benefit or pension book.

How to complain

Complaint procedures are similar to those of the Inland Revenue, leading ultimately to the agency head or an MP. An independent appeal mechanism for technical matters exists but is clumsy and not often used. The Revenue and Contributions Agency Adjudicator can also be asked to investigate complaints.

Summary
- Contact the right office.
- Always have the national insurance number and reference.
- Keep notes of all meetings and phone calls.
- Be persistent.

3

What to Tell the Inland Revenue

Tax legislation is complex. The following is a brief outline of disclosure requirements. Advice should always be sought in respect of any uncertainty.

Income tax

The general position is that most individuals living in the UK are liable to UK tax on their worldwide income. The tax system does have some specific exemptions.

The Inland Revenue require disclosure of all relevant information to allow them to properly assess liabilities. There are penalties for non disclosure even if a tax return has not been issued.

Income from employment: what needs to be declared?

- Salary, wages, fees, bonuses, overtime payments, commission, tips.
- Casual, spare-time, cash-in-hand payments.
- Cash allowances, shift allowances or allowances paid for early starts or late working, although some payments may be exempted.
- Statutory Sick Pay or Maternity Pay.
- Christmas bonuses including, for example, the value of gifts, hampers, alcohol and poultry. (Note: certain employees earning less than £8500 might not have to pay tax on non-cash items but they should still be declared.)
- Vouchers exchangeable for goods, commodities, services or cash.
- Expenses or bills paid on the individual's behalf or reimbursed — although a separate claim can be made for business expenses.
- Benefits — accommodation, car, fuel, private medical insurance, cheap or interest-free loans including overdraft facilities, free professional advice, use of company assets, for example, company

vans, mobile telephones and video equipment, or use of company chauffeur, gardener, and so on. (See Chapter 10.)

- Transactions under share option or profit-sharing schemes. (Certain payments, for example, profit-related pay and approved profit sharing schemes, are not taxable, but the return requires certain information.) (See Chapter 10.)
- Incentive awards and prizes.
- Lump sum payments in connection with the employment including statutory redundancy payments, ex-gratia sums, compensation. Although up to £30,000 of these may be exempt, they should still be declared. (See Chapter 11.)
- Earnings from work done abroad if the individual remains liable for UK tax. (See Chapter 14.)

Income from employment: what does not need to be declared?

- Annual staff functions up to £75 per annum per person, for example, a Christmas party or an annual dinner dance. (The limit before 5 April 1995 was £50).
- Luncheon vouchers up to 15p per day and canteen meals.
- Car parking facilities at or near the place of work.
- Routine medical check up or medical screening.
- Reimbursed expenses covered by a dispensation given to the employer. (See Chapter 10.)
- From 6 April 1995 allowances of up to £5 per night for personal incidental expenses when away from home overnight on business in the UK (or up to £10 per night for business trips overseas).
- Personal gifts from the employer, for example, a wedding present.
- Foreign Service Allowance paid by the Crown for extra cost of living abroad.
- Compensation for a loss of work done outside the UK where it has been agreed that the individual is not liable to UK tax. (See Chapter 14.)
- Gratuities from the Armed Forces (unless retired early, when the balance over £30,000 may be taxable).
- Certain lump sums or a refund of pension contributions from an employer's pension scheme.
- Sums an employer pays into a retirement benefit scheme or uses to buy an annuity on an employee's behalf.

Trading income: what needs to be declared?

The accounts should disclose all income from self-employment or partnership. Some additional matters not to be overlooked are:

- Grants — most are liable to income tax.
- Self-supply — if trading stock is taken for own use treat the supply as a sale at retail value.
- Payments in kind or where services or goods are received in exchange for services or goods of the business.
- Advertising gifts.
- Occasional receipts, for example, fees for writing an article for a newspaper. In addition, it is possible to be trading even though there is only one purchase and sale — take advice.
- Illegal trading receipts are taxable.
- Compensation or insurance proceeds may be taxable as an income receipt or as a capital receipt.
- Enterprise allowance, which should be shown separately on the tax return and not included in the accounts or turnover.

Trading income: what does not need to be declared?

- Detailed accounts need not be submitted if turnover was less than £15,000 in the year. (See Chapter 13.)

Pensions and state benefits: what needs to be declared? (see Chapters 7 and 12)

- Pensions paid by the State, or from a personal or company scheme.
- Pensions from abroad or from service in the Armed Forces.
- Unemployment benefit and Jobseeker's allowance.
- Income support when paid due to unemployment or strikes.
- Benefits from insurance policies where tax relief has been obtained on the premiums paid.
- State Incapacity Benefit taxable from 13 April 1995 subject to certain transitional rules after the first 28 weeks.
- Invalid care allowance.
- Industrial death benefit.
- Widowed mother's allowance.
- Widow's benefit.

Pensions and state benefits: what does not need to be declared? (see Chapters 7 and 12)

- State pensioner's £10 Christmas bonus.
- Child benefit.
- Student grants from local authority or school.
- Family credit or family income supplement.
- Guardian's allowance.
- Adoption allowances paid under schemes approved under Children's Act 1975.
- Attendance allowance.
- Disability living allowance.
- Severe disablement allowance.
- State sickness benefit to 13 April 1995.
- Wound and disability pensions to former members of Armed Forces.
- War widow's pension.
- Strike and unemployment pay from a Trade Union.
- Jobfinder's back to work grant.
- Earnings top-up (from Autumn 1996).

Property income: what needs to be declared?

- Income from letting property in the UK or abroad, including premiums on leases.
- Income from letting part of private residence, although rents up to £3250 a year for furnished accommodation in private residence may be tax-free. Certain details need to be declared. (See Chapter 15.)
- Income from a second home (for example, a holiday home). (See Chapter 16.)
- Income from any other property or land, for example, garage, field, sporting rights, fishing rights, ground rents, payments from utility company for poles, wires or cables, and so on.
- Furnished lettings and holiday accommodation.

Property income: what does not need to be declared?

- Contributions to household bills by partners or children.

Income from savings and investments: what needs to be declared?

- Interest from banks, building societies, savings accounts, solicitors, stockbrokers and so on, whether paid gross or net.
- National Savings Bank ordinary account. The first £70 (£140 if a joint account with spouse) is exempt but the full share of the income should be declared.
- National Savings Deposit, Income Bonds or Capital Bonds or investment account interest.
- Dividends from UK or foreign share holdings. Although UK dividends will be accompanied by a tax credit, which for taxpayers paying tax at the basic rate will cover their tax liability, it is still necessary to disclose this income.
- Shares received in lieu of cash dividends. (Take the details from the statement provided by the company but note that non-taxpayers are not entitled to a refund of the notional tax).
- Income distributions as shown on statements from unit trusts whether accumulated or reinvested. (Note: equalisation payments do not have to be declared but these reduce the cost of the units.)
- Mortgage interest or loan interest received from individuals.
- Interest on local authority bonds.
- Interest on company bonds and loan stock.
- Interest on government bonds, loan stock (gilts) or war stock.
- Interest on purchased annuities. (Note: the capital element is not taxable.)
- Gains on non-qualifying life assurance policies as advised by the insurance company.
- Accrued interest charged or rebated, for example, when certain stocks such as gilts are bought and sold. This is shown on the contract note.
- Income from abroad. (Note: different rules may apply for certain individuals born abroad or to foreign parents.)
- Income on capital provided by parents to their children who are unmarried and under 18 years of age where the income exceeds £100. (Note: income from certain National Savings products is exempt.)

Income from savings and investments: what does not need to be declared? (see Chapter 5)

- TESSA account interest unless the account is closed within five years.
- Personal Equity Plan income unless more than £180 in interest is withdrawn.
- National Savings certificates and index-linked certificates.
- Save As You Earn (SAYE) schemes.
- Premium Bond, National Lottery and gambling prizes.
- Interest awarded by a UK court as part of an award of damages for personal injury or death.

Other income: what needs to be declared?

- Beneficiaries of a trust or an estate should declare the income advised by the trustees or executors. (See Chapters 20 and 21.)
- Maintenance or alimony arising from a court order or legal agreement before 15 March 1988 (part may be exempted but the full amount received should be declared).
- Gains on the disposal of or switching of investments in certain off-shore roll-up funds.

Other income: what does not need to be declared?

- Maintenance under a first agreement which was made after 15 March 1988.
- Voluntary maintenance and alimony payments are tax free if legally unenforceable.
- Local authority home improvement grants.
- Most prizes and winnings unless connected with employment.

Capital Gains Tax
What needs to be declared?

- If the total value of assets disposed of in the year was less than £12,600 and chargeable gains were less than £6300 (1996–97) then full details do not have to be declared. Only tick the relevant box.
- If proceeds exceeded £12,600 or the gains were more than the annual exemption of £6300 (1996–97) then details of the gain or loss on each asset should be separately declared.

- Disposals to be declared include gifts, transfers and sales of shares, securities, property, land, leases, business assets, options, and so on.

What does not need to be declared?

- Private cars.
- Personal effects and goods worth less than £6000 when they were disposed of.
- Savings Certificates, Premium and British Savings Bonds.
- Gains from Personal Equity Plans.
- Bonuses from TESSA accounts.
- UK Government Stocks (gilts).
- Foreign currency for personal use.
- Betting winnings.

Summary

- With certain specific exemptions, all income and capital gains must be reported to the Inland Revenue.
- Failure to disclose can lead to penalties, or at worst, prosecution.
- If in any doubt seek professional advice or consult the Tax Office.

4

What Reliefs and Allowances Should be Received?

All taxpayers are entitled to some allowances that vary with personal circumstances. In addition tax law provides relief on certain expenses.

Personal allowance

All individuals, including children, are entitled to a personal allowance. For 1996–97 this is £3765.

Additional relief for children

A one-parent family may be entitled to claim this relief of £1790 for 1996–97 in addition to the personal allowance. To qualify, the relief is given if the child is living with a parent and is under 16 years, or if older:

- is receiving full time education; or
- is on a training course (including YTS) for at least two years.

If the child lives with both parents the allowance may have to be shared.

This special allowance can also be claimed by a married man if his wife is totally incapacitated by physical or mental infirmity throughout the entire tax year, and is given in addition to the married couple's allowance in these exceptional circumstances.

Since 6 April 1995 this allowance has only qualified for tax relief at 15 per cent.

Married couple's allowance

This allowance of £1790 (1996–97) is given in addition to the personal allowance where a married man is living with his wife. Since 6 April 1993 it has been possible for a wife to claim one half of the married couple's allowance, or the whole amount if her husband agrees.

The married couple's allowance can be increased where either party to the marriage has reached 65 years of age. Adjustments to the allowance are made in the year of marriage. The tax relief for this allowance is restricted to 15 per cent. Married couples can make the most of their allowances through careful planning. See Chapter 9 for details.

Age allowances 65–74 and 75 and over

Increased allowances can be claimed where the husband or wife will be 65 years of age during the tax year:

- The personal allowance can be increased to £4910 (1996–97) if the claimant is 65 years of age, and increased further to £5090 (1996–97) where the claimant will be 75 by the end of the year of assessment, provided that the claimant's income does not exceed £15,200.

- The married couple's allowance will also be increased to £3115 (1996–97) where *either* of the spouses is 65 years of age and again to £3155 (1996–97) where *either* of the spouses will be 75 by the end of the year of assessment. Again, the income of the individual making the claim must not exceed £15,200. Both these higher allowances only qualify for tax relief at 15 per cent.

The full relief will be given if the individual's total income is less than £15,200 for 1996–97. For every £2 of income above this limit the extra allowance is reduced by £1. However, allowances cannot be reduced below the basic levels. The income of the spouse is not taken into account when calculating this relief, each spouse having their own income limit.

Those qualifying for age allowances can make the most of them through careful planning. (See Chapters 9 and 12.)

Widow's bereavement allowance

In addition to the usual personal allowance (or the increased amount if over 65) widows are entitled to an extra allowance of £1790 for the year of bereavement and the next tax year as long as the parties were not separated before the time of death. The extra relief is withdrawn where the widow remarries. This allowance only qualifies for tax relief at 15 per cent.

Blind person's allowance

A registered blind person is entitled to an extra allowance. If both parties are blind they can each claim the allowance. If a blind spouse cannot use the full allowance because of low income the excess can be transferred to the other spouse. For 1996–97 this allowance is £1250.

Interest paid

Relief is available for interest paid on loans:

- to buy the family home in the UK (See Chapter 15);
- to buy UK property let at a commercial rent;
- to buy shares in or loan money to certain private companies;
- to buy an interest in a co-operative or employee controlled company;
- to lend to a partnership.

There are many conditions that must be met and advice should be sought where appropriate. In particular, care should be taken that interest is paid on a loan; not an overdraft, which is not allowable for the above purposes.

Pension contributions

See Chapter 12.

Charitable payments

See Chapter 18.

Private medical insurance

Since 6 April 1994 relief has been restricted to the basic rate of tax (24 per cent 1996–97) and is given by deduction from the premium where the insurance is for an individual, their spouse or another individual aged over 60.

Vocational training

Where an individual pays for their own training towards a national qualification they may get tax relief. The training organisation will be able to provide the details needed. From 6 May 1996 individuals aged over 30 are eligible in respect of retraining expenditure.

Maintenance or alimony payments

Payments to maintain children or divorced or separated spouses under court order or legally binding agreement can attract relief. Such payments include payments to the Department of Social Security to cover Income Support for separated or divorced spouses or the maintenance of children under a court order or Child Support Agency assessment.

Pre-15 March 1988 agreements qualify for tax relief but there are restrictions. Post-15 March 1988 agreements do not normally qualify for relief, except payments to spouses, which qualify for relief of up to £1790. This relief is restricted to 15 per cent.

Summary

- Carefully consider the reliefs and allowances that might be due for personal circumstances.
- Check these allowances are being given in the tax assessment or code number.
- If reliefs and allowances are not given then claim.

5
Tax-free Investing

There are several types of investment available which have some form of tax advantage. This may take the form of tax-free interest, tax-free capital growth or both. Opportunities to invest in a tax-free environment should be seized if they fit with the overall portfolio because tax erodes the return which an investor receives. It is also worth remembering that tax rates can go up or down and what may seem like a benign tax regime can suddenly become less friendly if a change of government or economic circumstances means that tax rates increase. Tax-free investments then become much more valuable to the investor.

Tax Exempt Special Savings Accounts (TESSAs)

Most banks and building societies offer a TESSA account. These are five-year accounts which, provided capital is not withdrawn during the five-year period, allow interest to be earned free of tax. Investors must be individuals aged 18 or over.

The maximum amount which can be invested is £9000 over five years. This breaks down into a maximum of £3000 in the first year and then a maximum of £1800 per annum for each of the following four years.

Interest can be withdrawn (net of basic rate tax deduction) during the five-year life but the capital must remain intact for the account to qualify as a TESSA. TESSAs do not have to be entered on a tax return but any withdrawal of capital causes all the interest earned to lose tax-free status.

On the maturity of a TESSA all interest earned thereafter will be taxable. Within a period of six months of the fifth anniversary of a TESSA it will be possible to open a second TESSA using, as an initial deposit, up to £9000 capital from the first TESSA. This second TESSA will continue to attract the same advantages and be subject to the same qualifications generally applicable to TESSAs. Those people who invest less than £9000 in the first year of their second TESSA can continue to save over the next four years in the usual way.

TESSAs are only suitable for taxpayers and because of their limited maximum investment are unlikely to form a major part of a sizeable investment portfolio. Nevertheless their advantages should not be overlooked.

When considering investing in a TESSA it is worth shopping around to find the best rate of interest payable. Rates on TESSAs change from time to time and a special deal may be available if a bank or building society is keen to promote its account. It is also worth checking that there is no penalty on closure of the TESSA during the five-year period. Usually no charges are made for running a TESSA.

Save As You Earn (SAYE) scheme

This government-sponsored savings scheme, operated by many building societies, was abolished in respect of new schemes with effect from 29 November 1994. Schemes existing at that date continue to enjoy the original tax-free benefits.

SAYE plans linked to approved employee share option schemes are unaffected.

Friendly society investments

Friendly societies are similar to insurance companies, in that they offer regular savings policies which pay out a guaranteed sum on death or a variable return on the maturity of the policy. Such policies are usually written for ten years and have the advantage that up to £270 per annum (£25 per month) can be invested per person in a fund which grows free of any tax. This tax advantage, together with sound investment management by friendly societies, has made the return to investors very attractive over recent years.

As a basic regular savings plan, friendly society policies can be considered by every investor. The return on death before maturity is low, so such policies are not a substitute for adequate life assurance.

National Savings

National Savings products have the great advantage that they are guaranteed by the government and are therefore an extremely secure investment. Several National Savings products are tax-free and these are examined below.

National Savings Certificates

These are issued on the basis of a fixed amount of interest being paid throughout a five-year term. Currently the 43rd Issue savings certificates pay 5.35 per cent per annum compound over the five years and the return is tax free. There is a maximum holding of £10,000 per individual on the 43rd Issue certificates with a further £20,000 being allowed for reinvestment of matured certificates from earlier issues. Minimum investment is £100.

Certificates are purchased either over a Post Office counter or by writing to the National Savings Office at Durham with an appropriate form which is available from any Post Office. Certificates can be encashed before the five-year maturity but the rate of return is reduced. These certificates are extremely attractive for higher rate tax payers because the return is tax-free. They are also a useful vehicle for making investments on behalf of children under the age of 18 because they produce no taxable income. They do not have to be entered on a tax return.

Index-Linked Savings Certificates

Similar to ordinary savings certificates in that they are a five-year investment, these certificates are, as the name implies, inflation proofed. The return on certificates is equal to the increase in the retail prices index (RPI) over the five-year period, plus a fixed additional amount of interest at maturity. For the 9th Index-Linked Issue the interest is 2.5 per cent per annum compound in addition to the change in the RPI on the five-year investment period.

As the investment return is tax-free these are extremely suitable for higher rate taxpayers. If inflation is likely to be high the returns from these certificates can be most attractive. They should always be considered as a safe 'each way' bet against inflation.

Similar maximum and minimum holdings apply as for the 43rd Issue fixed-interest certificates.

A point of caution is required with regard to the maturity of National Savings Certificates. If they are not encashed at the end of the five-year term they continue to earn tax-free interest but only at the general extension rate. This is a variable rate and is generally not attractive so care should be taken to encash or reinvest certificates promptly on maturity.

Children's Bonus Bonds

These offer a fixed rate of interest over five years with an opportunity to renew for further guaranteed returns on a five-year basis at the then applicable rate. No more returns are available after the holder attains 21 years of age. Minimum investment is £25. The maximum holding in the current Issue H is £1000. This is in addition to holdings of all other Issues of Children's Bonus Bonds.

Investments may be made for any individual under the age of 16 and these are ideal for gifts to children as no tax liability arises on the parents in respect of such a certificate.

The current rate of return is 6.75 per cent per annum compound.

National Savings Bank — ordinary account

This is effectively a bank account operated via the Post Office. Minimum investment is £10 and maximum £10,000. The first £70 of interest per individual per annum is tax-free. Income tax applies on interest above this level. The rate of interest is low and is varied from time to time.

Better returns can probably be found in building society accounts for large amounts of money but the tax-free status of the first £70 of interest makes this a useful account for children and other individuals who wish to receive gross interest. Higher rate tax payers may also wish to use the account, depositing sufficient capital to generate the £70 of tax-free income.

Premium bonds

A minimum of £100 to a maximum of £20,000 per person may be invested in this draw for tax-free prizes which range from £50–£1,000,000, but no interest is paid on bonds purchased. They may be encashed without penalty at any time, but are not eligible for prizes until held for one calendar month following the month of purchase.

Government stock (Gilts)

These are loan stocks issued by the government where both income and capital are guaranteed. They vary in maturity date, typically being categorised as short (up to 5 years) medium (5–15 years) or long (15 years plus) dated. The income payable on gilts is taxable along with any other income of the investor. Any capital gain made on the disposal of gilts is, however, tax-free. This means that gilts which pay a low income or 'coupon' can be particularly effective for higher rate taxpayers.

The price of gilts varies in the market, being either above, on or below their redemption price per £100 of stock. Thus it is possible to buy and guarantee either a capital loss or gain at maturity, depending on the price of the gilt at purchase.

Income is paid net of basic rate tax, which can be reclaimed by non-taxpayers. If gilts are bought through the National Savings Stock Register via a Post Office, the income is payable gross, which can be useful for non-taxpayers.

Particular note should be made of index-linked gilts which typically have very low coupons and most of the return therefore comes in the form of a tax-free capital uplift at maturity. For higher rate taxpayers this can be a most effective way of investing as these individuals will generally want capital growth rather than income. Index-linked gilts provide this in a very efficient and totally safe form. The government is unlikely to renege on repayment of gilts at maturity! The inflation proofing element of index-linked gilts can also be very attractive although potential returns must be compared with those available elsewhere and a judgement made about whether the return is likely to prove attractive in the period to maturity.

Other fixed interest bonds

There are a variety of fixed interest instruments available, many of which have complex tax treatments. These include Certificates of Deposit, Bulldogs, Treasury Bills and Permanent Interest Bearing Shares (PIBS). These instruments are quite specialised and are unlikely to be of interest to the majority of investors. They typically require very large minimum investments but may have the ability to produce a tax-free capital gain on encashment. Expert advice should be sought before these are considered seriously.

Personal Equity Plans (PEPs)

Personal Equity Plans were introduced by the government in 1986 initially to encourage investment in UK equities. PEPs provide for both income and capital gains to be exempt from any form of taxation. This makes them a very attractive form of investment.

PEPs take several forms and the most common of these are:

- Self Select Plans.
- Unit and Investment Trust Plans.
- Single Company PEPs.
- Corporate Bond PEPs.

Up to £6000 per person can be invested in a general PEP each tax year, with a further £3000 being invested in a single company PEP which can only hold the shares of one company.

Self Select Plans

These are typically run by stockbrokers and allow an investor to buy equities, and unit and investment trusts, within the framework of the stockbroker's PEP. The stockbroker then distributes dividends if required on a quarterly, half-yearly or yearly basis. The stockbroker typically charges a fixed fee or percentage of initial investment and an annual charge thereafter. The selection of such a plan should be made on the basis of whether income is required and how often the stockbroker will pay it out, together with careful consideration of the charges that the stockbroker will make. If commission-paying products such as unit trusts are to be bought via such a plan then consideration should be given to whether the stockbroker will rebate part of this or will keep all the commission.

Unit and Investment Trust Plans

The full £6000 per annum can be invested in qualifying unit and/or investment trusts. Qualifying trusts must be invested as to 50 per cent in UK or European Community company shares. Up to £1500 can be invested in non-qualifying trusts with the balance being in qualifying funds or direct equities or cash. The unit trust and investment trust plans are typically a PEP framework overlaying the basic investment. It is important to check and ensure that no additional charges are being levied for the PEP framework. It is also worth checking that there are no exit penalties should the PEP be encashed or transferred to another plan administrator.

Single company PEPs

In addition to £6000 in a general PEP, up to £3000 per annum can be invested into a single company PEP which buys shares of one company only. Many companies operate their own schemes to encourage wider ownership of their shares.

A PEP which is not performing satisfactorily can be transferred to another PEP provider, subject to any transfer penalties which might be levied by the transferring PEP provider.

Corporate bond PEPs

These allow for investments into certain corporate bonds, convertibles and preference shares up to the annual £6000 limit.

Property enterprise trusts

These schemes provide a means of obtaining tax relief for investing in commercial property. They are usually packaged so that the investor buys units in a property situated in a government-nominated 'Enterprise Zone', and the property is then let.

The investor can claim industrial buildings allowances and set these off against other income, and also receive the rental income for his share of the property.

Such arrangements can be attractive to people paying higher rate tax, as there is no limit on investment and thus it is possible to avoid the payment of any higher rate tax. They must, however, be seen as long-term investments which may be difficult, or even impossible, to sell if the property market does badly.

A minimum investment of several thousand pounds is required, and there is usually an option to borrow part of the total invested. Professional advice on the taxation and investment consequences of Enterprise Zone investment should always be sought.

Venture Capital Trusts

A Venture Capital Trust (VCT) is a quoted company which invests in shares of various unquoted companies. An individual will receive income tax relief at the rate of 20 per cent on a subscription for new ordinary shares in the VCT in respect of an investment of up to £100,000 provided the shares are held for at least five years. In addition individuals will be exempt from tax on dividends from VCTs and from capital gains tax when they dispose of shares in the VCT for investments of up to £100,000 a year.

Shares in a VCT may be used to defer the tax on a chargeable gain arising on the disposal of any other asset.

Enterprise investment scheme

The Finance Act 1994 introduced this legislation to replace the Business Expansion Scheme. This is designed to encourage investment in qualifying unquoted trading companies.

A maximum of up to £100,000 can be invested per tax year, giving tax relief at 20 per cent. Up to £15,000 will be available as a 'carry back' investment to the previous tax year.

Any capital gains on disposal of shares after 5 years will be tax exempt, and any losses will be relievable against income or capital gains tax. This has been an under-utilised scheme but tax reliefs have been extended to this investment. The tax on chargeable capital gains, arising from the disposal of assets on or after 29 November 1994, can be deferred where a gain is reinvested in an EIS. In addition, from 29 November 1994, the rule that not more than half of the market value of the EIS company's assets could be in land and buildings was abolished. This is likely to improve their attraction to investors.

Summary

- Consider opening a TESSA.
- Buy National Savings Certificates.
- Consider ordinary gilts for income.
- Consider index-linked gilts for growth.
- Use PEPs to hold shares/unit trusts.
- Take advice on Enterprise Zones, where a large liability to higher rate tax exists.

Particularly for the wealthy, risk-taking investor:
- take advice on Enterprise Investment Schemes and Venture Capital Trusts.

6
Should National Insurance be Paid?

National Insurance Contributions (NIC), originally introduced to finance state benefits such as healthcare, are in many eyes just another tax to be planned for. However, total avoidance is rarely the objective, as payment of NIC, unlike income tax, secures entitlement to various state benefits.

Contribution records and entitlement to benefits

The responsibility for collecting NIC falls to the Contributions Agency (CA), a section of the Department of Social Security (DSS). A person's NIC records are maintained by the CA using an individual's unique National Insurance number. This is normally issued before the 16th birthday and anyone who is employed, self-employed or who pays voluntary contributions should have already been notified of their own number. Anyone requiring a number should apply in person to their local DSS office.

Payment of contributions

For most individuals, the NIC with which they will be concerned are those deducted from their wages and salaries, commission and bonuses. These are known as Class 1 primary contributions and are accompanied by contributions by the employer known as Class 1 secondary contributions. Where a company car is made available for the employee's private use, the employer (but not the employee) pays Class 1A contributions on the value of the car benefit.

Self-employed individuals pay two types of NIC. The first, Class 2 contributions, is payable at a flat weekly rate and the second, Class 4 contributions, is calculated as a percentage of the person's taxable business profits.

These contributions are payable throughout an adult's working life (16–60 for women and 16–65 for men). An employee over pension age who continues working should provide an exemption certificate to his employer which is obtainable from the local CA office. This certificate does not affect the employer, who must continue to pay employer ('secondary') contributions.

Pension age for women has been increased to 65 for those born after 5 April 1955. It will be increased progressively from 60 to 65 for those born between 6 April 1950 and 5 April 1955.

In certain cases persons not otherwise liable for NIC may pay Class 3 voluntary contributions to qualify for benefits where their contribution record would otherwise be insufficient. Anyone considering the payment of Class 3 contributions to protect their entitlement to a state pension may find a pension forecast useful. This can be obtained by completing Form BR19, available from Social Security offices.

Contributions and the married woman

Marriage currently does not affect NIC, but certain married women who made the appropriate election before 12 May 1977 may be able to pay Class 1 employee contributions at a reduced rate and, if self-employed, avoid Class 2 contributions altogether. They will not be eligible to pay Class 3 voluntary contributions nor receive NIC credits and consequently are only entitled to a restricted range of benefits.

Employment contributions

Liability to Class 1 contributions is related directly to a person's earnings. NIC are not payable when earnings are below a lower earnings limit nor are they payable by employees on earnings above an upper limit. However, for employers there is no upper earnings limit for their contributions.

The rates of NIC and related earnings limits are usually adjusted annually and are set out in Chapter 22.

An employer providing a pension scheme for his employees which meets the required benefit levels, can elect to be 'contracted-out' of the state earnings-related pension scheme (SERPS). This election reduces employee and employer NIC from the higher 'contracted-in' NIC rates to the lower contracted-out rates.

An employee with an approved personal pension scheme can also opt out of SERPS. The DSS will subsequently pay various rebates into the appropriate personal pension.

The responsibility for the payment of both employee and employer contributions is that of the employer. The employer is entitled to recover the employee contributions through the PAYE system by deduction from the employee's earnings.

With the exception of company cars, most other benefits in kind which are non-monetary and are provided under a contract between the employer and the supplier do not currently attract NIC. Accordingly, payment of rewards by certain types of voucher or 'in-kind', for example, food hampers, can be free of NIC for employee and employer alike. Many schemes exist to avoid NIC but care should be taken, as not all have proved effective. As the authorities become aware of such schemes legislation is inevitably introduced to counter them.

Where a company car and possibly fuel is provided by an employer for an employee and is available for private use, the employer but not the employee must pay a further Class 1A contribution, for 1996–97 equal to 10.2 per cent of the appropriate Inland Revenue scale charge (that is the amount assessable to income tax on the employee as a benefit-in-kind).

Where an employee is outside the scope of benefits-in-kind legislation in respect of the private use of a company car, no liability to Class 1A contributions will arise.

Self-employment contributions

The basic Class 2 contribution has to be paid by all self-employed persons unless they have small taxable earnings (of less than £3430 for 1996–97). This relief must be claimed. Also excepted are persons not ordinarily self-employed (regarded by the DSS as those who have a regular job and whose earnings from spare-time self-employment would not be more than £800 per annum). For this relief, it is not necessary to obtain a certificate of exception.

Payment can be made quarterly in arrears on the receipt of a bill from the DSS or by direct debit.

In addition self-employed persons must pay Class 4 contributions which are 6 per cent (1996–97) of the assessable profits charged to income tax under Cases I and II of Schedule D between certain lower and upper limits. These limits, which are usually adjusted annually, are set out in Chapter 22. As from 1996–97 the tax deductible allowance of one half of the Class 4 contribution has been abolished.

These contributions are charged in the tax assessment for the relevant year which is raised by the Inspector of Taxes. They are normally paid with the income tax in two equal instalments.

Do not overpay contributions

Individuals who have more than one employment or self-employment, or who are employed and self-employed in the same year may end up paying NIC above the specified annual maximum in any one contributions year. Fortunately a repayment of these excess contributions can be claimed.

Employees who earn more than the upper earnings limit and pay maximum employee contributions in respect of that employment can elect for no employee contributions to be taken in respect of any other employment and, if also self-employed, for deferment of NIC on self-employed earnings.

NIC — employed or self-employed?

Generally, self-employed persons pay less NIC than employed persons. For example, for 1996–97 an employee with earnings in excess of £23,660 could pay 'contracted-in' contributions of £2112.24 while a self-employed person with similar earnings would only pay £1322.60. However, a self-employed person has lower benefit entitlements, and in particular may not be eligible for unemployment benefit.

The question of whether a person is employed or self-employed is not, however, a matter of preference but is based on the facts of each individual case. What must be determined is whether a person is employed under a contract of service (an employee) or performs services under a contract for service (self-employed). This is often a difficult question to answer. The fundamental test is whether the person performing those services is doing so as a person in business on his own account. These factors are also relevant to income tax treatment and some that may help to determine the employment status are set out in Chapter 13.

DSS leaflet NI 39 deals specifically with this subject for NIC purposes. There are exceptions to the general rule. The following persons are regarded as employees for NIC purposes despite the fact that they may actually be self-employed:

- Ministers of religion.
- Office cleaners.
- Certain persons supplied through agencies (for example, secretarial temps, nurses and supply drivers).
- Divers.

Special rules also apply to airmen, mariners and share fishermen. The DSS produces several leaflets on these specialised subjects.

Qualifying for benefits

The following table indicates which benefits may be paid on the basis of the various classes of contributions (provided that the requisite amounts have been paid). It should be noted that contributions under Class 1A and Class 4 do not purchase any benefits whatsoever.

Table 1

Benefits	Primary Class 1 'Contracted-in' and 'Contracted-out' standard rate	Certain married women/widow's reduced rate	Class 2	Class 3
Unemployment benefit — basic plus increase for dependants	Yes	No	No	No
Incapacity benefit — basic plus increase for dependants	Yes	No	Yes	No
State maternity allowance — basic plus increase for dependants	Yes	No	Yes	No
Retirement pension	Yes	On husband's contributions	Yes	Yes
Widow's payment	*Yes	On husband's contributions	*Yes	*Yes
Widowed mother's allowance	*Yes	On husband's contributions	*Yes	*Yes
Widow's pension	*Yes	On husband's contributions	*Yes	*Yes

*Only the husband's contributions can entitle a woman to widow's benefits.

Summary

- NIC liability depends upon employment status.
- The self-employed pay less NIC than employees but receive less benefits. Factors determining employment/self-employment are therefore of fundamental importance.
- An individual's NIC contributory record is critical to eligibility for various state benefits. A wife's entitlement will often depend upon her husband's record.

7

Which State Benefits are Taxable?

Taxable state benefits

Income tax legislation largely restricts the number of state benefits that are subject to tax. In practice, benefits that are payable to replace lost earnings, such as statutory sick pay and statutory maternity pay, are taxable. Those intended to meet specific needs of the claimant, such as child benefit, are not taxable. There is no general rule to work out if a benefit is taxable or not. The best way to approach the question is to refer to the following tables:

Table 2 *Taxable state benefits: Statutory Sick Pay (SSP)*

One rate applies per year

Average gross weekly earnings (£s)	Rates per week (£s)	
	From 6 April 1996	From 6 April 1995
58 or more	—	52.50
61 or more	54.55	—

Table 3 *Taxable state benefits: Statutory Maternity Pay (SMP)*

Average gross weekly earnings of £61 (£58, 1995–96) or more:	**Rates per week (£s) from**	
	6 April 1996	**6 April 1995**
Higher rate	90% of average earnings	90% of average earnings
Lower rate	54.55	52.50

SMP is not payable unless the woman:

- has been an employee for at least 26 weeks up to the 15th week before the baby is due, and
- her normal weekly earnings for the eight weeks up to the 15th week before the baby is due exceed £61 (£58 1995–96), and
- has reached 11 weeks before the expected week the baby is due.

Table 4 *Taxable state benefits: Unemployment Benefit*

Age	Rates per week (£s) from	
	6 April 1996	6 April 1995
Under State pension age (single)	48.25	46.45
Over State pension age	61.15	58.85

Note: Additions for child dependants are not taxable

Table 5 *Taxable state benefits: Retirement Pension*

Type of pension	Rates per week (£s) from	
	6 April 1996	6 April 1995
Basic		
Single	61.15	58.85
Wife (based on husband's contributions)	36.60	35.25
State earnings related/graduated	Variable	Variable

Table 6 *Taxable state benefits: Income Support*

	Rates per week
Paid to unemployed or strikers	Various

Notes: *(1)* Normally income support is not taxable, but the need for unemployed persons under 60 claiming this benefit to be available and actively seeking employment has led to it being taxable in that situation. There is a maximum which limits the total income support plus unemployment benefit which is taxable to the amount of the weekly unemployment benefit, plus the addition for an adult dependant.

(2) In practice, the unemployed over 60, single parents with children under 16 and someone at home caring for the severely disabled are not taxed.

(3) It is important that when the unemployed person receives a 'statement of taxable benefit' (either when ceasing claiming or at the end of a tax year) it is checked carefully. If no objections are made in writing within 60 days of the statement date then the amount shown as taxable cannot be disputed.

(4) Income support is also taxable if the claimant is one of a couple (married or not) and he (but not his partner) is involved in a trade dispute.

Table 7 *Taxable state benefits: Widows' Benefits*

Type of pension	Rates per week (£s) from	
	6 April 1996	6 April 1995
Basic (age 55 and over, others variable)	61.15	58.85
Widowed mother's allowance (child dependant additions are not taxable)	61.15	58.85

Table 8 *Taxable state benefits: other types*

Benefit	Rates per week
Industrial death benefit (if paid with retirement pension)	Various
Incapacity benefit – higher rate and long term	Various
Invalid care allowance (but not additions for child dependants)	Various

Note: The benefit rates per week are illustrations only and there may in certain circumstances be additions for dependants, spouses and/or children.

To avoid unnecessary administration in collecting tax on Social Security benefits, the Department of Social Security notify the Tax Office directly of benefits received by individuals on a tax year basis. This does not however remove the need for individuals to return these details on their tax returns.

In some instances, the Department of Social Security will deduct tax at source from incapacity benefit.

Non-taxable state benefits

Many state benefits are not taxable. The purpose of this book is not to give benefits advice but to draw attention to the tax consequences of taxable benefits. By way of illustration only, benefits that are currently not taxable include child benefit, family credit, housing benefit, state sickness benefit, state maternity allowance, attendance or mobility allowance and severe or disability living allowance. Both state sickness benefit and state maternity allowance are treated differently to the payments of SSP and SMP which an employer normally makes to an employee on the government's behalf. Only the latter are taxable.

Summary

- Not all state benefits are liable to tax.
- Generally, the benefits paid to replace lost earnings are taxable.

8
Life Assurance and Taxation

The main purpose of life assurance is to provide a sum of money when it is most needed, perhaps on the death of the family breadwinner or to repay a mortgage. In return for the premiums, a life assurance company undertakes to pay either a specified sum which may be increased periodically from its profits, or one which varies with the value of its investment funds. In many cases life assurance can also be a tax efficient investment.

Qualifying plans

Gains on life assurance policies are not normally taxed if such contracts are 'qualifying' life assurance plans or if they commenced before 19 March 1968.

A qualifying policy is one certified as such by the Inland Revenue, which usually requires the premium to be paid regularly, at least once a year, over a minimum ten-year period. It will pay out a minimum assured sum on death.

Individuals paying premiums on qualifying policies effected before 13 March 1984 will also benefit from tax relief of 12.5 per cent on the premium. In certain limited cases this tax relief can be recovered by the Inland Revenue.

An insurance company pays corporation tax and capital gains tax (both at 25 per cent) on the income and capital gains arising from its investment funds. Therefore insurance, as an investment, is more attractive to the higher rate taxpayer than basic rate taxpayer who might be better served by alternatives such as unit or investment trusts or personal equity plans (PEPs). (See Chapter 5.)

Provided the qualifying policy is maintained for ten years or three-quarters of the policy term the entire proceeds will be free of income tax in the hands of the plan holder.

Trusts

By writing insurance plans under trust, the proceeds need not necessarily form part of an individual's assets on his death. His intended beneficiaries/spouse might obtain the funds quicker than by waiting for probate, also removing such proceeds from his estate for inheritance tax purposes. Flexible trusts are available that enable trustees to vary the ultimate beneficiaries of the policy proceeds as needs require.

Types of policies

Term assurance

This is pure protection insurance where the sum assured only becomes payable if the person whose life is assured dies within a specified period of time. The term is fixed at the outset of the policy and should the individual survive to the end of the period no payment is made. The proceeds paid out are not liable to income tax but unless the policy is written in trust might be subject to inheritance tax.

Depending upon the use to which the policy is to be put the term assurance can be arranged to provide for an increasing or decreasing level of cover over the policy term and for renewal at the end of the policy period, or conversion into other forms of assurance along the way.

Family income benefit

This is a term assurance policy providing for the payment of a fixed sum at regular intervals following the date of death of the assured until the expiry date of the plan. These plans can secure high tax-free benefits for relatively low premiums as the overall risk to the life assurance company decreases each year.

Endowment

An endowment policy is an insurance arrangement for a specified period with the tax-free sum assured payable on survival to the end of the term or prior death.

Such endowment policies are usually either 'with profits' or 'unit linked'. 'With-profit' endowments provide for the sum assured to be increased by regular bonuses declared by the insurance company from its profits. Such additions may be an annual reversionary bonus and/or a possible terminal bonus on maturity of the policy.

'Unit-linked' endowments provide for the premiums to be invested through the insurance company funds into unit trust funds. The sum payable at maturity will reflect the value of the units held.

Low cost endowment assurance

These policies are a combination of endowment and term assurance. The period of the contract is fixed and should the life assured die within the term the sum assured becomes payable. However the sum assured is also payable if the policyholder is living at the end of the period. These contracts are widely promoted and used as security for home loans offered by banks and building societies.

Maximum investment plans

A ten-year qualifying unit-linked endowment with minimal life cover. Such plans provide the investor with a greater choice of investment funds compared with the traditional with-profits fund.

Whole of life assurance

This offers a permanent form of life assurance with no fixed term. The benefit becomes payable on the death at any time of the life assured. Such contracts can be written with or without profits. The with-profit policy attracts bonuses that are added to the plan while non-profit policies simply provide a sum assured.

Low-cost whole of life plans combine with profits and decreasing term assurance.

Investment-linked whole of life plans provide life cover and an element of saving. There is a choice of life cover between a maximum and minimum level which is normally maintained for ten years. Thereafter the level of cover is dependent on investment performance. Premiums for whole of life contracts can be payable throughout the policyholder's life or may be arranged for a particular term or age, depending upon the individual's circumstances.

Single premium insurance bonds

These bonds are non-qualifying insurance policies providing minimal life cover protection and maximum investment opportunity. Such bonds can provide a capital growth opportunity over the medium term for both basic and higher rate taxpayers. It is possible to derive a form of regular income by withdrawals from the bonds and these can be effectively tax-free. A tax charge might arise on withdrawals in excess of 5 per cent per annum, or on final disposal of the bond or death of the investor.

Friendly Society plans

See Chapter 5.

Dread disease/critical illness cover

This pays a lump sum on diagnosis of a specified illness, for example, cancer, heart attack, stroke or permanent disability. Most policies are non-qualifying and are potentially liable to higher rate tax.

Permanent health insurance

This provides a regular payment in the event of an individual being unable to work through incapacity, by sickness or accident. Benefits become payable after a deferral period ranging from 4–104 weeks. Benefits are payable until the insured is able to resume work or reaches retirement age. Provided premiums are maintained the policy cover cannot be withdrawn by the insurance company.

Back to back arrangements

This is generally a combination of a temporary life annuity where payments fund a ten-year qualifying life policy. After ten years the value of the annuity is transferred to the life policy. The arrangement provides certain tax advantages and the proceeds of the qualifying policy can be taken free of tax.

Discontinuing the policy — options

If an endowment/whole of life policyholder is unable or does not wish to maintain the premiums he has the option to surrender the plan. However, due to administration charges there is unlikely to be any significant return within the first few years of the contract. The higher rate taxpayer might also be subject to a tax charge on early surrender within the specified period for a qualifying policy.

The plan could be made paid up, in which case premiums cease but the plan remains in force for the original term. The sum assured under the policy would be reduced to reflect the total of the premiums actually paid.

Finally there is a secondhand market available for existing plans. The policy should have run for at least ten years or half its term. Auction houses invariably offer a higher return than the policy surrender value.

Divorce

A court can make any order it deems fit regarding future ownership of any of the assets of a marriage, including a life policy. Divorce does not cancel the interest of any named persons so if a spouse is the assured, a life assured, a trustee or beneficiary this continues but practical problems could arise.

Joint life policies in particular can be a problem and the options available should be considered at the time of the divorce. Care should be taken where a spouse is an unnamed beneficiary, for example, if the policy is worded 'on trust for my wife absolutely' then divorce would destroy the original beneficiary's interest and the policy would revert to the estate of the life assured until remarriage.

General

On 1 October 1994 an insurance premium tax was introduced at a rate of 2.5 per cent of the gross premium. The tax applies to most general insurance policies including sickness and accident and private medical insurance.

Legislation is to be introduced to exclude insurance benefits from tax where they become payable if the person entitled to them is sick, disabled or unemployed.

This will include benefits which are payable during convalescence or rehabilitation, or to top up earned income when it is reduced following sickness, disability or unemployment.

However, if an employer has a group insurance scheme to meet the cost of sick pay for employees or where policy premiums have received tax relief this change will not apply.

It should be noted that widespread changes in the taxation of life assurance policies are proposed and may be introduced later this year.

Summary

- Life assurance should form the cornerstone of a financial plan, providing protection against death or prolonged illness.
- While insurance contracts can be used as an investment vehicle, greater tax efficiency might be achieved through other forms of investment.
- Insurance policies should be considered a long-term commitment, as surrender in the early years might result in either a loss of premiums or a charge to tax.
- The range of available insurance contracts should provide a solution to most people's requirements.

9
Marriage

Husbands and wives are each treated as an independent taxable individual. A married couple living together does, however, remain relevant as a unit for various tax purposes.

The married couple's allowance

A legally married couple living together has its own separate married couple's income tax allowance. Temporary separation, because of sickness, for example, or where someone is working abroad, does not affect this. The married couple's allowance is first of all available to the husband, but if he does not have taxable income and is unable to use the allowance, it can be claimed by his wife. The allowance can also be transferred from the husband to the wife, even though he has taxable income, by written notice from both of them to the Inland Revenue. The notice is to be made using Inland Revenue Form 18 obtainable from the local tax office. This has to be dealt with before the beginning of the tax year and applies to all future years until notification is given for it to be withdrawn. It is also possible for a wife to claim half of the allowance, without the agreement of her husband, if she sends a simple written request to the tax office. In addition, where a husband is found to have insufficient income to use all, or part, of the allowance, he may transfer it to his wife using Inland Revenue Form 575 for each year this is done. The claim for the transfer is to be made within six years after the end of the tax year.

Gifts of assets may be made between husband and wife without capital gains tax or inheritance tax liabilities, although there is a limit for inheritance tax where either the husband or wife is not domiciled in the United Kingdom. Gifts, however, between parents and children are not so exempt.

Marriage

In the year of marriage, the married couple's allowance is reduced proportionately the later the marriage takes place in the tax year. A claim for this to be transferred from the husband to the wife can also be made in that first year. The personal tax allowance cannot be transferred between husband and wife. Attention should be given to the possibility of moving investments, including building society deposits, that produce taxable dividends and interest, to the spouse who can make the best use of the personal tax allowance. In addition, by transferring investments between spouses, the income may be taxed at a lower rate. For example, investment income taxed at 40 per cent received by a husband may only be taxed at 20 per cent if instead it were received by his wife, thereby giving an overall advantage to the married couple. It must be realised that to do this the asset producing the income must be given by one spouse to the other, without restriction.

Other factors, nothing to do with taxation, may affect changes of this sort. Where it is not appropriate to transfer investments from one to the other the assets can be placed in the joint names of the husband and wife and an Inland Revenue Form 17 completed so that, for tax purposes, the amount of income is divided between them according to their ownership shares. This sort of claim, which is known as a declaration, applies to income received immediately after the date of the claim. There are problems in doing this with bank deposit accounts and building society deposits held in joint names. Form 17 states that a declaration may not be made for these assets where the income is split equally. However, it can be done for other assets such as stocks and shares.

Income tax relief, at 15 per cent, is available for house mortgage interest on loans up to £30,000. The relief can be shared between the husband and wife as they choose regardless of which of them pays the interest. Here, an Inland Revenue Form 15 is to be completed and sent to the tax office within twelve months of the end of the tax year to which it is to apply.

End of marriage — separation and divorce

Where a married couple has separated and it is likely to be permanent, the whole amount of the married couple's allowance remains available for the year when the separation happened, but it cannot be claimed thereafter. If there are children then whoever takes them will be entitled to an additional personal allowance. The amount of the married couple's allowance must, though, be deducted from this allowance if they are available to the same person. If there are children living with both parents then two allowances might be available, one for each parent.

For inheritance tax, the exemptions referred to above remain available even though the couple has separated. The exemptions cease on divorce, from the date of the final decree.

Court Order maintenance payments between separated or divorced couples, including arrangements under the Child Support Agency rules, qualify for income tax relief to the payer, up to an amount equal to the married couple's allowance. There is no tax charge on the person receiving the maintenance income. No relief is available for maintenance paid direct to a child, though Court Order payments made between parents for the maintenance of a child do attract relief. This relief, also, is no more than equal to the married couple's allowance. These rules apply to all new Court Orders. Payments still being made under arrangements entered into prior to various dates in June 1988 are treated more generously and require separate attention.

On remarriage, either parent may be entitled in the year of marriage to the additional personal allowance. A father cannot also claim the married couple's allowance in his year of remarriage. As this is restricted depending on the date of the marriage in the tax year, it may be preferable for him to claim the full additional personal allowance in the year of remarriage rather than the married couple's allowance.

End of marriage — death

Although a widow is entitled to a bereavement allowance in the year of death of her husband and for the following year, there is nothing similar for a man whose wife has died.

Cohabitation

With more than a third of marriages ending in divorce, cohabiting or remaining single are real possibilities. These have their own tax implications needing careful attention.

For tax purposes the individuals will continue to be treated as separate persons. UK tax legislation does not recognise the state of common law wife and common law husband.

Each person will have their own personal tax allowance but only one additional personal allowance will be available in respect of any children.

Tax relief is available for house mortgage interest on loans up to £30,000 as for a married couple but the claim can only be made by the payer. The relief is linked to the residence rather than to the individual, so it is not possible to obtain relief for more than one total amount of £30,000 for the same residence. Relief can be shared between the individuals in proportion to the amounts of the separate loans they may have. There are favourable rules for mortgages taken out before August 1988. These advantages could be lost where changes in circumstances are being considered. Specialist advice should be taken.

Where marriage occurs, and a child of the couple is living with them, it is usually better for the father to claim additional personal allowance in the year of marriage in respect of the child rather than the married couple's allowance. This is because the married couple's allowance is reduced by one-twelfth for each month ending before the date of marriage, whereas the additional personal allowance is given is full.

Gifts of assets passing between people living together will be subject to capital gains tax and inheritance tax. Inheritance tax is also applicable on death in such circumstances; there being no exemption for people cohabiting. The usual annual exemptions referred to in Chapter 19 are, though, fully available.

Single person status

A single person is entitled to a personal tax allowance, with house mortgage interest relief on a loan of up to £30,000, at a rate of 15 per cent. An additional personal allowance is also available for a child living with a single person. If there is more than one child, no more than one tax allowance is available.

Children

The child is an individual in its own right with its own personal tax allowance. There are restrictions to prevent relief from being claimed where a child's income, amounting presently to more than £100 a year, is derived from its parents. This does, though, give an opportunity for grandparents and others to provide a child with qualifying income for this purpose. Tax might then be repayable to the child but a claim for this must be made to the tax office. Where it is possible for parents to give their children significant amounts of money then investments that do not produce taxable income, such as National Savings Certificates and Friendly Society Baby Bonds, should be considered. Where appropriate, professional advice should be obtained for a simple form of settlement known as a 'bare trust' to be arranged. This can have worthwhile advantages, cost little and need not be complicated.

Wills

The importance of having a will cannot be overstated, particularly in the context of the family. The lack of a will at an already difficult time can be a source of unnecessary distress and the result can seem to be surprisingly unfair. This is dealt with more fully in Chapter 21.

Summary

- Ensure that the Tax Office is promptly notified of changes in circumstances, and claim all available reliefs.
- Spread the ownership of income between husband and wife to maximise income tax allowances and the lower bands of tax.
- Give careful thought to family affairs and plan in advance of significant events, so that maximum use is made of the annual capital gains tax and annual inheritance tax exemptions.
- Do not forget that children have their own tax allowances and should be included in any planning.
- Make sure that every adult in the family has made a will, which is reviewed regularly.

10
Employment Benefits and Incentives

Employees, including directors, are taxed on their emoluments. These include all earnings, perks and profits arising from their employment, whether paid by the employer or someone else. Reimbursed expenses (other than those exempted by an employer's dispensation) are taxable subject to a business expenses claim.

In addition to being taxed on regular salary or wages, other items such as tips paid by customers or sales commission paid by the employer are also taxable. The employer will deduct tax from the commission; the onus is on the employee to declare the tips.

Not all earnings, however, are in cash; some are in kind and there are detailed rules for the taxation of items received as benefits in kind.

The most common benefits in kind are the company car and medical insurance. Other examples would include holidays, loans, the private use of company assets such as boats, living accommodation and many others.

The taxation of these depends, primarily, on earnings. Employees earning at the rate of less than £8500 per annum, including benefits, are taxed only on the secondhand value of what they receive. So it can be beneficial for low-paid employees to be paid by the company with a free holiday that cannot be encashed or with clothing or household utensils where the secondhand value is very low. Considerable care is necessary if it is proposed to take advantage of these rules.

For directors and employees earning over £8500, tax on benefits in kind is generally by reference to either a scale charge, as with cars, fuel, company vans and mobile phones, or by reference to the cost to the employer of providing the benefit. There are detailed rules to suit specific circumstances.

The House of Lords' decision in the case of *Pepper* v *Hart* in November 1992 held that, where appropriate, the cost to the employer is only the marginal or additional cost of providing the benefit, for example, where a fee-paying school provides a place for a teacher's child on terms which do not displace others, the taxable benefit is just the cost of additional items such as books, food and so on, and not the whole cost of fees.

There may be a deferral of tax liability by receiving a benefit in kind rather than in cash. The advantage of a true benefit in kind is that, although liable to income tax, it may not attract National Insurance contributions (NIC) although the employer, but not the employee, is now liable to NIC (Class 1A), on the benefit of cars and fuel.

Benefits, even if taxed, are useful incentives for employees but there are other more tax-efficient ways of rewarding employees.

Share incentives and options

Company share schemes allow directors and employees to participate in the growth in value of the company they work for. They provide an incentive to employees, particularly when favoured by tax benefits, and can be an effective and efficient way for the company to reward its employees and/or directors.

The main types of scheme, both approved and unapproved, are as follows.

Unapproved share schemes

Shares are issued to the employees, who pay full market value. There is normally no tax liability on the employees until the shares are sold, when any capital gain is taxed in the normal way.

If the price paid for the shares is less than market value, the discount or undervalue is taxed as earnings on the employee. Similarly, if the shares are sold for more than market value, the excess is taxed as earnings.

There are special rules to catch suddenly manipulated changes in share value.

There are additional, complex, rules relating to shares acquired pre-26 October 1987.

Approved profit sharing schemes

The essence of these schemes is that the company gives a yearly tax-free allocation of a prescribed value of shares to employees.

The value that can be provided each year to an employee is limited to the higher of £3000 or 10 per cent of salary, subject to an overriding maximum of £8000.

All full-time employees who have served a qualifying period must be eligible to participate. Employee shareholders in certain private companies who, together with others connected with them, control 25 per cent or more of the company are ineligible to participate.

The scheme cannot discriminate between employees, and all must participate on similar terms, for example, pro rata by reference to salary and length of service. The scheme is described as profit sharing but no actual sharing of profit need be involved.

The schemes provide the employee with deferred remuneration in a tax-efficient manner. The shares cannot be sold in the first two years.

On the sale of the shares, no income tax liability arises if the shares have been held for five years. The 1996 Finance Bill proposes to reduce this to just three years. Capital gains tax is calculated in the normal way — on the difference between the value when acquired, plus indexation, and the sale proceeds.

Assuming no other gains in the year, the capital gains tax annual exemption would be available to set against the taxable gain.

Alternatively, from 1 January 1992, shares in an approved profit sharing scheme can be transferred, within six weeks of acquisition, to a single company Personal Equity Plan up to a value of £3000 and can then be held free of income tax and capital gains tax.

Employee share ownership plans (ESOPs) and employee benefits trusts (EBTs)

An ESOP is a structure involving a share or share option scheme and an EBT.

The EBT is used to facilitate the share scheme. It is funded by the company, which would look for corporation tax relief on its contributions. The funds can then be used to buy or subscribe for company shares, so that shares are available for the scheme, and an internal market created to enable employees to sell scheme shares.

Share option schemes

A share option is a right to acquire shares in the future at a favourable price. If the shares rise in value, taking up the option (ie by exercising it) permits shares to be acquired effectively at a discount to their market price. If the employee wishes, the shares can be sold immediately at a profit.

By contrast, if the shares fall in value, the option can simply be ignored.

The mere granting of an option does not normally trigger a tax liability. See below for a description of various option schemes.

Unapproved share option schemes

If options are issued to employees outside one of the approved share option schemes, no tax charge arises on the grant of the option, unless it can be exercised more than seven years later.

Where the option is for less than seven years and is not exercised, there is no tax liability unless any payment is received for giving up the option.

When the option is exercised, there is an income tax charge on any excess of the market value of the shares at that time, over the price paid for them. The market value of the shares at the date the option is exercised is the amount used to calculate any capital gain on a future sale of the shares. Indexation allowance (see Appendix A) is also calculated by reference to this amount.

There are special rules to charge income tax on manipulated increases in value.

Approved executive share option schemes

The tax favourable status of these schemes was withdrawn as a result of unfavourable publicity, particularly regarding options granted in privatised utilities.

Options already granted under the old rules before 17 July 1995 may continue to be exercised.

The rules for exercising these options are the same as for company share option plans (see below) which are the replacement for the executive schemes.

Company share option plans

These replace the approved executive share option schemes from 17 July 1995. Very similar rules to the old scheme except the value of the employees' options are limited to £30,000 and the shares cannot be issued at a discount.

The membership of these schemes can be restricted to particular employees and directors and those included do not need to be treated on the same terms. Those who are included have the opportunity to accumulate capital sums on favourable tax terms.

There is no tax charge on either the grant or the exercise of the option.

A capital gains tax charge can arise on the subsequent sale of the shares on the difference between proceeds and cost plus indexation.

Options may be exercised between three and ten years from grant and not more than once every three years. Exercise at other times will give rise to income tax liability.

Savings related share option schemes

The detailed conditions for the approval of these schemes is broadly the same as for approved profit-share schemes. In particular, discrimination between employees is not permitted except on the basis of earnings, length of service and similar.

The essence of these schemes is that the options are issued to employees to acquire shares in the company at a future date at a price fixed at the grant of the option. That price can be at a discount of up to 20 per cent of the market value of the shares at the time the option is granted.

The employee then saves through a Save As You Earn (SAYE) contract (see Chapter 5) with a bank or building society to buy those shares (maximum amount £250 per month).

At the end of the SAYE contract, five or seven years hence, either the option shares are taken up or if they have dropped in value, the SAYE saving can be kept. New three year saving schemes are proposed from Spring 1996.

The only tax liability normally on the employee would be a capital gain on the eventual sale of the shares taken up. As from 1 January 1992 the shares can be transferred to a single company PEP, as for shares under an approved profit-share scheme.

Profit Related Pay (PRP)

An attractive alternative to share schemes, which does not involve the complexities of share issue and ownership but still links the employee to the success of the company, is profit-related pay (PRP).

As its name indicates, PRP is a fluctuating part of an employee's earnings which is formally linked to the profits of the business or the part of the business in which he or she works. The purpose of an approved PRP scheme is to allow employees to obtain a tax saving, subject to certain limits, in relation to payments made under the scheme.

Payments made under an approved PRP scheme are exempt from income tax, although the relief does not extend to NIC.

The maximum tax-free remuneration for an employee from a registered PRP scheme is £4000 or 20 per cent of total pay, whichever is less.

Total pay excludes benefits in kind, superannuation and payroll charity contributions and includes the PRP paid for the year concerned.

For someone receiving the full amount of PRP, there could be an annual tax saving of £1000 for a basic 25 per cent taxpayer or £1600 for a higher rate 40 per cent taxpayer.

For a PRP scheme to be approved it must provide for a part of the business' profits to be allocated as PRP (the PRP pool) and this PRP pool must then be shared out between all employees (with limited exceptions) with each employee sharing in the pool on similar terms. Certain shareholder directors cannot be included.

A PRP scheme must be registered with the Inland Revenue in advance if it is to achieve tax relief.

Almost all private sector businesses can apply to have a PRP scheme registered for tax relief. Broadly speaking, an application can be made if the employer is in business to make profits.

A scheme must relate to an employment unit, which is either a whole incorporated or unincorporated business in the private sector or a distinct part of such a business. Special rules apply to a head office or research department.

New recruits and part-timers can be excluded but at least 80 per cent of the other employees in the employment unit must be covered by the PRP scheme.

PRP is paid at least once a year on the basis of audited profits. It can be calculated on an interim basis as often as desired and paid weekly, monthly or quarterly.

Summary

- Taxable income from employment includes benefits in kind as well as cash.
- Share ownership and incentive schemes offer tax efficient returns for employees.
- An approved profit-related pay scheme offers tax-free earnings.

11
Redundancy

The tax position of termination payments made by employers to employees who are redundant or lose their job in circumstances other than death or injury is complex. Specific professional guidance is usually advisable.

The basic rule is that statutory redundancy payments and non-statutory compensation payments are exempt from tax to a maximum of £30,000, with any excess being taxed as income in the normal way under Schedule E, provided that there is a genuine redundancy or loss of office.

If there is a legal right to receive a payment upon termination of employment, or payment is received for past services, it will be taxable in full under Schedule E. Similarly, the Inland Revenue take the view that if an employer habitually makes compensation payments upon termination of employment, thus giving an employee an expectation of receiving such a payment when his employment ceases, such a payment became contractual by implication and is therefore taxable in full.

The Revenue have, however, stated that in practice the £30,000 exemption will be available where habitual compensation payments are made under a non-statutory redundancy scheme in the case of genuine redundancy.

Statutory redundancy payments

Subject to certain conditions and limits, an employee is entitled by law under the Employment Protection (Consolidation) Act 1978, to receive a payment from his employer upon being made redundant. The basic rules are as follows:

1. The employee must have a minimum of two years' continuous employment.

2. For each year of employment in which the employee was aged 41 or over, 1.5 week's pay is allowed.
3. For each year of employment in which the employee was aged 22 or over, but which does not fall within (2) above, one week's pay is allowed.
4. For each year of employment in which the employee was aged 18 or over, but less than 22, half of one week's pay is allowed.
5. A week's pay is currently subject to a maximum of £205.
6. The maximum number of years of employment to be taken into account for this purpose is 20.

It can be seen from the above that a statutory redundancy payment will always be under the £30,000 exemption limit.

Non-statutory redundancy payments

The Inland Revenue have indicated in a new Statement of Practice, published on 17 February 1994, that lump sum payments made under a non-statutory scheme in addition to, or instead of, statutory redundancy pay will only be liable to tax if they exceed £30,000. This will be the case whether the scheme is a standing one which forms part of the terms on which the employees give their services, or is an ad hoc scheme devised to meet a specific situation such as the sudden closure of a particular factory.

However, the Revenue is 'concerned' to distinguish between payments under non-statutory schemes which are genuinely made to compensate for the loss of a job through redundancy, and payments which are made as a reward for services carried out by the employee during the course of his employment, eg a payment which is conditional on continued service in the employment for a time will be regarded as a fully taxable terminal bonus if it is calculated by reference to any additional period served following issue of the redundancy notice; similarly payments made for meeting production targets or doing extra work in the period leading up to redundancy are examples of terminal bonuses subject to tax.

The Revenue have confirmed their willingness to allow employers to submit proposed non-statutory redundancy schemes or, in the case of an existing scheme, details of a proposed lump sum payment, to them for advance clearance that payments up to the £30,000 limit are exempt from income tax.

Compensation payments when employment ends

It is worth repeating that a compensation payment for loss of office provided for by the terms of a contract of employment will be taxable in full. Where this condition does not apply an employee is entitled to the benefit of his contract of employment, whether this is written or verbal, and if the employer terminates the contract in breach of its terms the employee is entitled to compensation. The amount of compensation will depend on matters such as the period of notice to which the employee is entitled and whether or not there has been unfair dismissal. In most cases such compensation will fall within the exemption.

Where an employer pays a sum of compensation in excess of the amount to which the employee is entitled, any such excess is an ex-gratia payment.

There are potential difficulties with the Inland Revenue where an ex-employee signs an undertaking not to sue the employer for wrongful dismissal. In some cases the Inland Revenue argue that the compensation payment is taxable in full as having been received for the agreement to a restriction of future conduct rather than for the loss of office. Professional advice is recommended to challenge this line of attack.

Ex-gratia payments

An ex-gratia payment to a departing employee is one which the employer is under no legal obligation to make. It may arise because the employer wishes to pay more than the legal entitlement or where there is no legal entitlement to compensation at all. An ex-gratia payment made on genuine redundancy or loss of office will normally fall within the exemption but with two important exceptions:

1. Where it is customary for an employer to make such a payment when an employment ends, even though there is no legal obligation to make it, the Inland Revenue take the view that it is taxable. For example, a lump sum based on the length of service which it is an employer's established policy to pay on termination of employment.

2. A payment made on retirement, or in anticipation of retirement, is taxable as income in full under the pensions legislation and is therefore outside the exemption. However, a payment made to an

older employee due to genuine redundancy or in circumstances where he is sacked or forced to resign, will not normally be regarded as a 'retirement' payment.

This tax treatment is highly subjective as the employee is at the mercy of the Revenue regarding a payment in anticipation of retirement. The Revenue have already stated, for example, that a termination payment to a long-serving senior officer aged 60 upon leaving to take a similar job elsewhere may well be regarded as a 'retirement' payment which would not therefore qualify for the exemption.

Pay in lieu of notice

In the Inland Revenue's view, the payment of wages in lieu of notice is taxable in full if it is paid to an employee under his terms and conditions of employment, ie where the contract of employment specifically provides for a payment in lieu of notice to be made. In addition, if it is customary for the employer to make such payments to outgoing employees, even though the employee has no legal right to the payment, the Inland Revenue take the view that it is taxable as it has effectively become part of the conditions of employment leading to the employee's expectation to receive such a payment.

If the employer terminates the employment in breach of contract, eg by failing to give the employee the notice to which he/she is entitled, any resulting payment will not be taxable subject to the £30,000 limit. A true non-taxable payment in lieu of notice is therefore one where the employer pays the employee for leaving without working the normal notice period and without the employee taking legal action for what would have been received if the period of notice had in fact been worked.

This is a developing, and contentious, area of the law and professional advice is recommended.

Tax relief for termination payments

An important consideration for the employer is the question of whether or not tax relief will be obtained for making a termination payment.

The payment of statutory redundancy and similar sums by an employer are allowable by law as a deduction from business profits. If such payments are made on cessation of the business, the rules enable the employer to pay up to three times the statutory redundancy payment and, where payment is made after the business has actually ceased, it is regarded as having been made on the last day of the business.

There is no specific law which permits a deduction for other termination payments and these are judged on their own merits. Provided it can be shown that a payment is of a revenue nature and is incurred wholly and exclusively for the purposes of the business, it will be allowable against profits.

Payments as compensation for loss of office usually qualify as they are made under a legal obligation in the interests of the business, for example when the purpose is to get rid of an unsatisfactory employee.

A similar principle applies to ex-gratia payments but it can be more difficult to obtain a tax deduction where there is no legal obligation to make such a payment. As it is essentially voluntary in nature, the employer has to convince the Revenue that it is still made for business purposes only. In practice, reasonable payments are usually allowed by the Inspector as relating to staff welfare in the sense of maintaining goodwill between the remaining workforce.

Tax relief for an ex-gratia payment made to a director/shareholder may be denied on the grounds that it is a distribution of profit and not a business expense. Similarly there may be problems in obtaining relief where a payment is made in connection with the takeover of a company.

Other points

Upon leaving an employment, there is only one £30,000 exemption per employee available and all the termination payments are aggregated for this purpose.

A payment in excess of £30,000 should be reported by the employer to the Inland Revenue within 30 days of the end of the tax year in which it is made.

Where a part or all of a termination payment is taxable, it is treated as received for tax purposes on the date of cessation of the employment and not, if different, on the date it is received. This can affect the rate of tax to be paid in respect of the payment as it is added to an employee's other taxable income for the year in question.

A termination payment does not relate only to the receipt of money. It also includes the market value of any assets given by the employer, for example, if an employee is given a company car as part of the severance package.

Physical payment of the termination payment to someone other than the employee, at his direction, is still treated as belonging to the employee.

To the extent that payments exceed £30,000, the employer is required to deduct PAYE from the excess. If payment is made after Form P45 is given to the employee, tax is deducted at 24 (1996–97) per cent but if payment is made before Form P45 is given to the employee, the taxable part must be taxed according to the employee's PAYE code number and a higher rate of tax may initially be paid in excess of true liability. Repayment of such excess tax would then have to be formally claimed back later.

Summary

- The tax treatment of payments on loss of employment is not straightforward.
- £30,000 tax exemption available in certain circumstances.
- Changing Inland Revenue attitudes — professional advice is essential.

12
Planning for Retirement

There are currently about 10,000,000 retired people in the UK — around one in five of the population. By the year 2000, it is expected that the proportion will rise to one in four. The 'third age' can now be expected to last two or more decades after retirement. Given the increasing numbers of retired people and the dwindling population in paid employment paying taxes to fund state benefits, it makes sense to plan for retirement. As with all things, the earlier the start, the better.

Basic retirement pension

At state pensionable age (currently 60 for women and 65 for men) the government pays a basic retirement pension based on the National Insurance contributions (NIC) record accumulated over a working life. The pension is usually about 20 per cent of national average earnings and each year is increased in line with inflation. Each individual qualifies for a basic retirement pension if they have a full NIC record for about 90 per cent of their official working life, currently defined as 44 years for women and 49 years for men, so it is important to have paid full contributions or be granted exemptions or credits for, at present, 40 years (women) or 44 years (men) to receive the full pension. Voluntary (class 3) contributions can be paid to make up an NIC record if necessary.

It should be noted that the government has now legislated that equalisation of the state pension age at age 65 will take effect from the year 2020. The equalisation process will be gradually phased in over a period of ten years, commencing in the year 2010.

Women are credited with NIC under the 'Home Responsibility Protection' scheme if they are not in paid work but receive child benefit for children under the age of 16; this scheme can also apply to carers of people receiving attendance allowance. The basic rate of pension for 1996–97 is £61.15 per week for qualifying individuals. A married woman whose NIC record is insufficient for her to qualify for a pension in her own right may still get a pension based on her husband's contribution record. The rules are complicated and advice should be sought. The basic married woman's retirement pension for 1996–97 based on her husband's contributions is £36.60 per week when he is aged 65 or over. There is also a (tax-free) £10 bonus at Christmas, and an extra 25p per week when the pensioner is over the age of 80.

It is possible to find out how much pension can be expected on retirement by asking for Form BR19 'Retirement Pension Forecast' from the nearest Department of Social Security or Benefits Agency office. A check can be made of how many qualifying years' contributions have already been accumulated, how many can be expected to be made by retirement and if it is worthwhile making up for missing years by the payment of voluntary contributions.

State Earnings Related Pension Scheme (SERPS)

This scheme was introduced in 1978 to give employees an earnings-related pension to top up the basic retirement pension. Given the present ageing population, government forecasts indicated that SERPS was likely to prove increasingly expensive, so the benefits to be paid under the scheme are to be reduced for people retiring from the year 2000 onwards.

Within limits, for a member of SERPS, the more that is earned over a working life the higher the addition to the basic retirement pension. However, many people are 'contracted out' of SERPS, either through their employer's occupational pension scheme or a personal pension scheme of their own. They will only receive the basic retirement pension when they retire, but they should be more than compensated for the absence of SERPS by the pension they receive from their employer or personal pension scheme. The government provides financial incentives to contract out of SERPS and increase private pension funding, thus reducing the financial burden on the state.

Supplementing state benefits

A combination of the full basic state pension and maximum SERPS entitlement is unlikely to be sufficient to ensure a standard of living to which people will have become accustomed. A tax efficient way of supplementing state benefits is through membership of an employer-sponsored occupational pension scheme or a personal pension plan. In broad terms, under both types of arrangement personal contributions within certain limits are tax deductible, employer contributions are tax deductible and the fund in which contributions are invested grows free of tax.

Occupational pension schemes

Many employees are members of pension schemes set up by their employer. The employer must contribute to the scheme and often employees will also contribute a fixed percentage of salary to the scheme, although some schemes, particularly in the public sector, are non-contributory. It cannot be compulsory for an employee to join their employer's scheme but in many cases it is in the employee's best interests to join rather than make their own private pension provision, as in this case employers are unlikely to contribute.

New members of occupational pension schemes since March 1989 are subject to the 'earnings cap'; this means that only the first £82,800 (1996–97) of earnings are allowed to be pensionable.

Occupational pension schemes come in two main categories:

- Final salary
- Money purchase

The differences are very marked, so it is worth checking the rules to find out in which category the employer's scheme belongs.

Final salary schemes

In a final salary scheme, the pension is related to the number of years the individual has worked for the employer and the salary in the last years of service. 'Final salary' can be defined in a number of ways. These schemes are usually based on $1/60$ or $1/80$, although other fractions are used.

Example

Mr X retires after 20 years' service on a final salary of £15,000 and is a member of his employer's $\frac{1}{60}$ scheme. His pension would be:

$20 \times \frac{1}{60} = \frac{1}{3} \times £15,000 = £5000$ per annum

The Inland Revenue do not allow occupational schemes to pay pensions of more than $\frac{2}{3}$ of final salary. That means 40 years' service for a $\frac{1}{60}$ scheme and 53 years' service for a $\frac{1}{80}$ scheme; it is perhaps unsurprising that over 99 per cent of the population do not receive the maximum pension of $\frac{2}{3}$ final salary when they retire!

Retiring employees in private sector final salary schemes can normally choose to 'commute', that is give up some of their pension at retirement in exchange for a lump sum. The lump sum is tax-free, unlike pensions which are taxed as earned income, so this is usually a sensible thing to do. The absolute maximum lump sum the Inland Revenue allow is 1.5 times final salary after 20 years' service. Not many people will have been in a scheme long enough to qualify for this. The amount that is often paid is $\frac{3}{80}$ of final salary per year of service.

Example

With 20 years service Mr X qualifies for a maximum tax-free lump sum of:

$20 \times \frac{3}{80} = \frac{3}{4} \times £15,000 = £11,250$

Commuting the pension for immediate cash means that the annual pension payable would be reduced. The Inland Revenue needs to agree the basis on which commutation is calculated for a particular scheme, but as a rough guide, a man retiring at 65 would potentially give up £1 of pension for each £9 of cash he takes.

Example

By taking the maximum cash of £11,250 Mr X could see his pension reduce from £5000 to £3750 per annum

Public sector schemes such as the Civil Service and National Health Service pension schemes are set up on a statutory basis and normally offer a pension build-up of $1/80$ of final salary for each year of service and a non-optional tax free lump sum often calculated as $3/80$ of final salary for each year. In practice this gives a value which is in line with a private sector $1/60$ scheme.

It must not be assumed that an occupational pension will increase automatically every year in line with inflation. This luxury is only enjoyed by members of public sector schemes and the very best company schemes. However, in 1990 the government introduced legislation whereby most final salary schemes had to provide pension increases in line with rises in prices, but only for service after 1990 and only if there were surplus funds. Apart from that, most schemes pay increases only at the discretion of the pension fund trustees.

Final salary pension schemes will normally include an entitlement to a spouse's pension. This means that if the scheme member dies, either before or after retirement, then a reduced pension will be paid to the surviving spouse.

There have been various test cases concerned with pensions taken to the European Court of Justice in recent years, including *Barber v Guardian Royal Exchange* and the Coloroll Case. The general thrust of the European Court decisions in these and other cases is that pension rights should be considered in the same way as pay and employers should not discriminate between men and women where entitlement to an occupational pension is concerned. In particular, schemes should not have different pension ages for men and women.

Members of a final salary scheme which will not pay the maximum pension allowed by the Inland Revenue at retirement (the majority of people) should seriously consider paying Additional Voluntary Contributions (AVCs). A member can pay AVCs as an addition to their employer's scheme or to a 'Free Standing' AVC scheme (FSAVC) with an insurance company or other organisation. Members of public sector schemes are often also eligible to buy 'added years' of service in the scheme by means of AVC payments. In any event, this is a means of building up a fund which can be used to boost the pension on retirement. In most cases they will be established on a money purchase basis even if the main pension scheme is of the final salary type; 'added years' will however increase final salary benefits. The Inland Revenue do not however allow the total benefits from an occupational scheme and

AVCs/FSAVCs to exceed the maximum limits mentioned previously, ie a maximum pension at retirement of $2/_3$ the final salary.

AVCs started after April 1987 cannot be used to boost the lump sum at retirement, only the pension. AVCs are a very tax-efficient form of saving. Income tax relief is granted for AVCs and in fact for employee pension contributions up to a ceiling of 15 per cent of earnings (including benefits in kind), the fund building up tax-free until retirement. If the 15 per cent contribution ceiling is not used in a particular year it cannot be carried forward; it is lost.

However if FSAVCs totalling more than £2400 gross in any tax year are paid, the Inland Revenue will carry out a 'headroom check' to ensure that the maximum figure of $2/_3$ the final salary is not exceeded, and may put a restriction on the amount of FSAVCs that can be paid.

Transferability

A member of an occupational pension scheme who leaves service with two or more years of membership has a legal right to a preserved pension. A preserved pension is what has been earned during the period of service and will be paid at normal retirement date. As an alternative to a preserved pension, all leavers after 31 December 1985 are legally entitled to elect for the cash value of their pension rights to be transferred to another employer's pension scheme, a personal pension plan or a buy-out bond. The latter is a type of individual policy offered by a number of life insurance companies. The major objective in effecting such a transfer is to achieve a higher level of benefits than might be payable under the existing scheme.

For members of final salary occupational pension schemes, the decision of whether or not to transfer can sometimes be complex, particularly where a transfer to a personal pension or buy-out bond is being considered. Consequently, anyone contemplating such a course of action should always seek expert advice.

In addition to transfers from occupational pension schemes, it is possible to transfer between various other types of pension arrangements. Once again, expert advice should be sought on the appropriateness of such transfers.

Money purchase schemes

As the name suggests, these schemes work by building up a pot of money which is then used to purchase a pension on retirement. Some occupational schemes, and all personal pension schemes, operate on a money purchase basis. The contributions made by an individual, and their employer, if relevant, accumulate in a personal tax-free fund.

Contributions within limits set down by the Inland Revenue qualify for tax relief and any growth on the money in the fund is not taxed. On retirement, the fund is used to buy an income for life. This is known as an annuity.

Under a money purchase scheme, the amount of pension depends on how much is in the fund at retirement and what form the pension is taken in. For example, it is possible to decide to take a smaller initial pension which will increase annually at a fixed percentage rate, instead of a level pension which will remain unchanged throughout life; the pension might continue until the death of both spouses instead of stopping on the pensioner's death. Part of the pension fund may be taken as a tax-free lump sum leaving a reduced amount to buy an annual pension.

Flexibility is the key to money purchase schemes, but at the expense of the guarantees that final salary schemes provide.

Example

Mr X retires in January 1996 at the age of 65 having accumulated a fund of £100,000 under a money purchase pension scheme. His wife, Mrs X, is aged 60. If Mr X decides to take pension only with no tax-free cash sum he has a number of possible choices:

Level pension for Mr X's life only per annum	£11,172
Pension for Mr X's life only increasing by 5 per cent per annum — starting level	£7716
Level pension payable until second death of Mr and Mrs X per annum	£9005

Source: Investment Intelligence

As can be seen from these illustrative figures it pays to give careful consideration to how pension benefits are taken from a money purchase scheme.

Personal pensions

Personal pensions were introduced in July 1988 to replace retirement annuity policies. Until then, the latter had traditionally been used for the purposes of private pension provision by both the self-employed and employees in non-pensionable employment. It should be noted that those with existing retirement annuity policies are allowed to continue paying regular contractual premiums as well as (normally) additional single contributions.

As with FSAVCs, personal pension providers include banks, building societies, friendly societies, unit trust companies and insurance companies.

All personal pensions are established on a money purchase basis whereby the ultimate benefits are dependent upon contributions paid and investment growth achieved thereon. Contributions build up inside a tax-free fund which is then used to provide benefits at retirement. In the past this fund has had to be used to purchase an annuity as soon as benefits commence to be paid but it is now possible for personal pension holders to defer annuity purchase until maximum age 75 and make withdrawals directly from the pension fund, within limits set out by the Government Actuary. This option is normally only suitable for those with larger pension funds, say in excess of £100,000.

Contributions to a personal pension plan may be made by anyone under the age of 75 who has 'net relevant earnings'. Broadly, this is taxable income from employment or self-employment. The maximum percentage of net relevant earnings which may be paid varies with age and currently ranges from 17.5 per cent at age 35 or less to 40 per cent between age 61 and 74. In addition, the amount of net relevant earnings upon which contributions may be made in any tax year is restricted by the earnings cap (1996–97: £82,200). It is interesting to note that the earnings cap does not apply in respect of contributions paid to existing retirement annuity policies. However, the limits on contributions to retirement annuity policies only range between 17.5 per cent and 27.5 per cent of net relevant earnings, depending upon age. Where contributions are paid to both a retirement annuity policy and a personal pension in any tax year, the earnings cap once again applies.

Contributions to personal pension plans for employees in non-pensionable employment may be paid (within the specified limits) by both individuals and/or their employers. Personal contributions paid by such employees are made net of basic rate tax relief. Any higher rate relief may subsequently be reclaimed through the individual's local Tax Office. Employers' contributions are also tax deductible but the specified limits relate to the total of employer and employee contributions.

Self-employed persons are not allowed to pay contributions net of basic rate tax and must therefore claim all tax relief directly from the Tax Office.

If contributions paid by an individual in any tax year are less than the permitted maximum, any balance may be carried forward to future years. This balance is known as 'unused relief' and may be carried forward in all cases for up to six years.

In addition, contributions paid in one particular tax year can be carried back to the previous tax year and thereby allowed for tax purposes in that previous tax year. Where an individual has no net relevant earnings in the previous tax year, the contribution may be carried back two years. It should however be noted that contributions paid by an employer may not be carried back to a previous tax year.

In contrast to an occupational pension scheme, there is no limit on the pension which may be paid under a personal pension plan. There is however a limit on the amount of tax-free cash which may be taken. This is restricted to 25 per cent of the accumulated fund at retirement.

Contracting out — personal pension plans

Employees who are not contracted out of SERPS under an employer's occupational pension scheme may effect a personal pension plan for the purpose of contracting out. These plans are known as appropriate personal pensions. Under this method of contracting out, both employee and employer pay full rate NIC. The appropriate rebate (plus a government incentive payment and tax relief on the employee's part of the rebate) is subsequently paid into the individual's personal pension account. Although an incentive payment for contracting out is no longer applicable to occupational pension schemes, holders of contracted out personal pension plans who are aged 30 or over on 6 April in a tax year are entitled to a bonus, which will be available until 5 April 1997. This is equivalent to 1 per cent of earnings between the lower and upper earnings limit for NIC purposes.

The benefits under such a plan cannot be drawn until state pension age. In addition, the accrued fund must be used to purchase a pension only. Consequently, no part of the fund can be taken as a tax-free cash sum.

Investments and taxation

On retirement, taking the tax-free lump sum from the pension scheme combined with the accumulated nest egg of a working life gives a lump sum of capital to invest to boost retirement income. Unfortunately, the Inland Revenue do not spare the retired investor.

The basic retirement pension is taxable, as are pensions from occupational and personal pension schemes. The Inland Revenue are slightly more generous to over 65s with increased age allowances (see Chapter 4). As noted previously, an individual's total income (before allowances) in a tax year has to be less than £15,200 to get the full increased allowances.

If pensions total less than £15,200 a year, it may be worth trying to keep the level of investment income down so that total income does not go over the limit. Tax-free investments (see Chapter 5) could be considered to help keep inside the income limit.

Boosting retirement income in a tax efficient manner can be achieved through Purchased Life Annuities (PLAs), particularly where a tax-free lump sum has been taken from the pension scheme. In exchange for a lump-sum investment, an insurance company promises to pay an income for life, so PLAs are not a good idea for people with short life expectancies. The Inland Revenue treat part of the income payment received as a return of part of the capital invested, and thus not liable to tax, and part as taxable income. Such an arrangement could help in avoiding the age allowance trap where income is close to the £15,200 danger mark. However, this is at the expense of the capital.

Example

If Mr X were to spend £10,000 of his life savings on a Purchased Life Annuity in January 1996 when he is 65 years of age then he could expect to receive an income for life of £1072 per year. However, only £527 of this amount would be taxable.

Source: Investment Intelligence

Summary

- Ensure full contributory record for state retirement pension.
- State pension unlikely to be adequate — consider private provision through membership of employer scheme or take out personal plan.
- Consider AVCs to meet pension shortfall.
- Invest for retirement in a tax-efficient manner.

13

Self-employment — The Tax Breaks

For those willing to take the plunge into the entrepreneurial world of self-employment, there can be considerable taxation advantages, particularly when contrasted with the tax rules affecting employees.

First, whereas an employee has tax and National Insurance contributions (NIC) deducted at source from earnings, a self-employed individual has the distinct cashflow benefit of paying these liabilities in instalments, often many months after the end of the period in which the profits were earned.

Secondly, the Inland Revenue conditions for allowing expenses as deductions from taxable income are often far less stringent for the self-employed.

Both of the above factors offer considerable tax planning opportunities for the self-employed, and they will be examined in more depth later in this chapter. However, one of the consequences of having such advantages is that the Inland Revenue do look carefully to see whether an individual is actually self-employed for tax purposes.

Is it really self-employment?

Before looking in more depth at the taxation consequences of self-employment, it is important to determine whether the status of the individual is indeed self-employed as opposed to employed. Although in the majority of cases the distinction between the two is obvious, there are occasions where there can be some doubt.

Whilst there is no definition of 'self-employment' in tax legislation, Inland Revenue practice and legal cases have given some guidelines.

The following circumstances would point towards self-employment:

- The individual's own money is involved and is, therefore, at risk in the business.

- The individual decides how the business is run.
- The individual decides on the hours that are worked.
- The individual provides the equipment/tools necessary to perform the work and is responsible for correcting any mistakes.

Conversely, the following factors would indicate an employee status:

- Set hours are worked and are paid by the hour, week or month.
- The work must be done by the individual; that is, a substitute is not allowed to be provided.
- The individual is not responsible for meeting any losses incurred in the business.
- The individual is paid holiday and sick pay and is a member of the firm's pension scheme.

Starting up

When commencing in business, the following administrative tasks should be performed to ensure that tax affairs are kept in order:

- A previous employee should send Form P45 from their last employer to the local Tax Office.
- The local Tax Office should be informed that a new business has commenced. There is usually a requirement to complete an Inland Revenue Form 41G, which will give the Tax Office all the necessary information.
- The local office of the Department of Social Security should be informed, for NIC purposes.
- The local VAT Office should be contacted to register for VAT if taxable turnover (sales) exceeds certain specific limits. From 29 November 1995, these limits are as follows:
  — turnover in the next 30 days will exceed £47,000; or
  — turnover in the past 12 months exceeded £47,000 (this limit should be reviewed on a monthly basis).
  It is also possible to register for VAT on a voluntary basis, even if the above limits are not exceeded.
- Accurate, up-to-date records of the business should be kept to enable accounts to be prepared in due course.

How are the self-employed taxed?

Once in business, the self-employed will pay tax on their agreed taxable profit less tax allowances. The tax will be collected through notices of assessment issued by the Tax Office.

If annual turnover is less than £15,000, the Tax Office will accept a simple summary of trading income less business expenses, as opposed to more detailed accounts.

Example

Simplified tax accounts, often described as 'Three Line Accounts' would be in the following form:

	£
Turnover/Trading Income	14,270
Less: Business Expenses	(5,015)
Net Taxable Profit	9,255

The Tax Office will assess profits in respect of each tax year. For businesses set up before 6 April 1994, once they had been assessed for three tax years of assessment, then profits were taxed on what is known as the 'Preceding Year' basis. This means that those businesses were taxed for each tax year on the profits of the accounting period which ended in the previous tax year.

Example

Accounting period – year 30 June 1993

Profits would be assessable in the 1994–95 tax year, with the tax payable in two instalments on 1 January 1995 and 1 July 1995

Under this system, the most effective choice of accounts year end date for cash flow purposes was 30 April, as this produced a 20 month gap between the year end and the date of payment of the first instalment of the resultant liability.

The change to the current year basis of assessment

However, with effect from the 1997–98 tax year onwards, there is to be a new system of taxing the profits of the self-employed. From this tax year, profits will be assessed on a 'Current Year' basis instead of the 'Preceding Year' basis as mentioned above.

Tax payment dates will also change, as tax will be payable on an individual's total income and capital gains on 31 January following the tax year (interim payments will be payable on 31 January in the tax year and 31 July following). This tax will be due without any assessment from the Inland Revenue, so it will be the individual's responsibility to calculate the correct amount of tax if interest charges are to be avoided.

Although many factors could influence the most beneficial choice of year end under the new system, there is still likely to be a cashflow advantage of choosing a year end that occurs early in a year of assessment.

Example

The accounting period ended 30 April 1998 would be assessable in 1998–99

but:

The accounting period ended 31 March 1998 would be assessable one year earlier in 1997–98

These new rules have applied to all businesses which have started since 5 April 1994. For continuing businesses trading prior to 6 April 1994, the last tax year under the old rules was 1995–96. The 1996–97 tax year will therefore be the transitional year between the two systems.

Example

Year of Accounts	Tax Year of Assessment
30 June 1994	1995–96 'Preceding Year' Basis
30 June 1995 ⎱ x 12 months 30 June 1996 ⎰ 24 months	1996–97 'Transitional Year'
30 June 1997	1997–98 'Current Year' Basis

As the 'Transitional Year' will include profits relating to more than one accounting period, it would appear beneficial to increase income and reduce expenses during these periods, as opposed to the prior or following accounting periods. This is because only a 12 month proportion of the periods in the 'Transitional Year' will actually be assessed to tax. The relevant legislation contains provisions to counter any manipulation of the rules to reduce tax liabilities in this way, and these should be borne in mind before any action is taken. Indeed the Inland Revenue measures are sufficiently widely drawn arguably to catch quite innocent changes in business behaviour. It is desirable that professional advice be sought in relation to this whole area.

National Insurance contributions

Self-employed individuals are liable to pay both Class 2 and Class 4 NIC. This is looked at in more detail in Chapter 6.

What expenses are allowable?

As mentioned earlier, the tax rules relating to allowable expenses for the self-employed are considerably less stringent than for employees. This difference springs from the different wording of the tax legislation on this subject.

For the self-employed, an expense need only be incurred 'wholly and exclusively' for the purposes of the trade. However, an employee must satisfy the Tax Office that an expense has been incurred 'wholly, exclusively and *necessarily* ' in the performance of his duties of the employment in order to be allowable for tax purposes. Although the wording is indeed similar, the small difference enables the self-employed individual to cast a much larger net when considering which expenses can be claimed.

Broadly speaking, expenditure is either Revenue or Capital.

Revenue expenditure

Revenue expenditure is perhaps best described as expenses relating to day-to-day matters and, where these are incurred 'wholly and exclusively' for the purpose of the trade, they are generally allowable in full for tax purposes.

Examples of revenue expenditure include:

- Heating costs.
- Rent of premises.

- Employees' wages (where it can be justified, an individual may consider employing their spouse to obtain an allowable deduction in respect of the wages).
- Interest paid on borrowed funds used in the business.
- Leasing costs of expensive items of machinery, and so on.

Despite the availability of most revenue expenses as a deduction from profits, there are certain expenses which do not qualify for relief. The most common of these is entertaining, which is disallowable in full.

While on the subject of revenue expenses, pre-trading expenditure can be claimed as a deduction from profits. Broadly, any revenue expenses incurred during the seven-year period prior to the commencement of trade which would normally be allowable for tax purposes, are allowed as a deduction from profits in the first year of assessment.

Since 30 November 1994, certain expenses incurred following the cessation of a business have been able to be utilised against income or capital gains of the tax year in question.

Capital expenditure

In general terms, expenditure is of a capital nature when it involves either the acquisition of, or significant alteration to, assets which are used, or are to be used in the business.

Examples of such expenses include the acquisition of new machinery, legal expenses relating to the purchase of a capital item or even the cost of 'repairs' on an item where the value of that item is enhanced.

Capital expenditure is not allowable as a deduction from taxable profits. However, such expenditure often qualifies for capital allowances — a special system where an allowance is granted to compensate the business for the fall in value of a capital asset used in the business. The rules governing capital allowances can be quite complex and, therefore, they are not covered in any detail in this guide. Broadly, a trader can claim an annual allowance of 25 per cent of the capital cost of plant and equipment on a reducing balance basis.

Example

	£	Claim £
Year 1		
Cost of item of plant	7000	
Capital Allowances due (25%)	(1750)	1750
'Written down' cost	5250	
Year 2		
'Written down' cost		
brought forward	5250	
Capital Allowances due (25%)	(1312)	1312
'Written down' cost	3938	

Private/domestic expenditure

As stated above, revenue expenditure is usually allowable as a deduction from taxable profits as long as it has been incurred 'wholly and exclusively' for the purpose of the business. Such a description, however, does not cover a self-employed individual's private expenditure, and it is important that any such expenditure is not claimed as an allowable deduction. Any such 'expenses' of the business, for example the wages paid by a self-employed businessman to himself, are deemed instead to be drawings from the business.

Some expenditure can relate to both business and private use. Whether such expenditure is of a capital nature (for example, the purchase of a car) or of a revenue nature (for example, home telephone bills), it is important that the business proportion is identified as accurately as possible, and only this proportion deducted from taxable profits.

In the case of a car used both for business and privately, this will necessitate the keeping of some form of mileage record to enable the correct business proportion to be calculated (in this respect, it is important to note that journeys made between an individual's home and his regular place of work are deemed to be for private purposes only).

Similarly, where the individual will be undertaking some or all of the business activities from home, there is an opportunity to claim an estimate of expenses incurred in the home for business purposes, although care must be taken in relation to capital gains tax on the eventual sale of the home (see Chapter 15).

Where an individual is trading in partnership, there may be the further possibility of the partnership paying rent in respect of one of the rooms in the house and claiming it as an expense. Once again, any advantage should be weighed against losing part of the capital gains tax exemption on the home.

Trading in partnership

Before entering into any partnership, careful consideration should be given to the fact that partners agree to become jointly and severally liable for each other's debts of the partnership. As such, it is an extremely serious commitment which should not be undertaken lightly.

Using business losses

Although the last thing in mind in starting a business is the possibility of making a trading loss, it is wise to prepare for the possibility. It is very likely in a new venture that various factors combine to produce a situation where the business makes a loss. A prime example of this in recent years has been the recession which has pushed many previously profitable businesses into a loss position.

While no-one wants to make a loss, the pain is eased somewhat by being able to deduct tax losses against other income and thereby obtain a tax refund or a reduction in another tax liability.

In general terms, tax losses suffered by a business can currently be used in the following ways:

- Treated as a deduction from other income of the year of the loss, or of the next year.
- Treated as a deduction from the future profits of the same trade.
- Treated as a deduction from the capital gains (for instance on the sale of shares) of the year of the loss, or of the next year.

Additionally, for a loss incurred in the first four years of a business, there is the opportunity to 'carry back' the loss, and to deduct it from other income of the previous three years, thereby obtaining a tax repayment. Similarly, when a business ceases, there is the chance to carry back any loss suffered in the last 12 months of the business against the profits made by the same trade in the previous three years.

Under the forthcoming 'Current Year' basis of assessment rules, trading losses will be available to set against other income of the previous tax year to the extent that they are not utilised against other income of the same year. Any losses still remaining would then be carried forward to set against future profits of the same trade.

Summary

- Consider the implications of the change from the 'Preceding Year' to the 'Current Year' basis of assessment.
- Ensure that all revenue expenses are claimed, including the business element of motoring and domestic expenditure.
- Ensure that capital allowances are claimed, where available, for capital expenditure.
- Use any business losses to obtain a tax refund or reduce tax liabilities.

14
Working Abroad

There is much mystique about taxation and working abroad, fuelled by comments such as 'tax-free salaries'. The only certainty is that tax will be a crucial factor affecting the major aspects of working abroad such as length of stay, where to live, what to do with the UK home, pensions, medical expenses and savings.

While this chapter will concentrate on the UK tax reliefs and planning opportunities available through working abroad, it is important to remember that the country to be visited will also have its own tax rules, which must be allowed for. Unfortunately, those countries in which 'tax-free' salaries can be earned are becoming fewer all the time.

The general rule

A person living and working in the UK who goes abroad for occasional visits (holidays and short business trips) will be considered respectively 'resident' and 'ordinary resident' in the UK and liable to UK tax on worldwide income and gains. This general rule may be slightly altered if the person does not have UK 'Domicile' — a status determined by birth and long-term intentions; particularly the place where someone anticipates dying.

The three terms, 'resident', 'ordinarily resident' and 'domicile' can be seen to have very different tax meanings to their normal use in connection with property — a frequent source of confusion in correspondence between individuals and the Tax Office. See Appendix D for a discussion of these terms.

It is assumed throughout that the individual working abroad is UK Domicile, having been born in the UK of parents also born here and who intends to return to the UK. Specific advice should be sought in other circumstances.

Period spent abroad

The UK tax relief and the scope for tax planning available to an individual through going abroad depends on both the length of time spent outside the UK — the longer the period the more the opportunities available — and the reason for going.

For periods abroad of longer than a tax year, the objective is usually to become 'not resident' and 'not ordinarily resident' and so be only liable to UK tax on earnings from duties performed in the UK and, subject to other available tax reliefs, on income from UK investments.

For shorter periods overseas, the aim is to remove the overseas earnings from UK tax and to claim maximum relief for any overseas tax paid.

Leaving the UK

If an individual goes overseas under a full-time employment contract where either all duties will be performed abroad or any UK duties will be incidental, and the period of absence will include a complete tax year with return visits to the UK of less than three months per year on average, then that individual will be regarded as 'not resident' and 'not ordinarily resident' by Revenue practice.

This status can be confirmed by completing a Revenue Form P85 which, if accepted by the Inland Revenue, will enable them to issue a UK employer with a notice permitting salary and wages to be paid without tax deduction.

The above does not apply for self-employed persons and other individuals leaving the UK where the 'residence' and 'ordinary residence' usually will be determined at the end of a three-year period when all facts (for example, sale of home, return visits) are known.

It should be noted that the Inland Revenue continue to have regard to the availability of accommodation in deciding whether a person has permanently or temporarily left the UK.

When a person leaves the UK, there are no provisions for splitting the tax year. However, by concession, the Revenue will normally regard an employee as 'not resident' and 'not ordinarily resident' from the day following departure. This concession can be important where large capital gains are expected on investment sales, since the deferral of the contract of sale until after departure may save significant tax. Care must be taken with such planning as the Inland Revenue will withdraw the concession where it is blatantly abused. Also, remember that sales after taking up residence in a new country could leave the gain or income liable to higher overseas tax.

Working abroad as a non-UK resident

Income from duties abroad will not be liable to UK tax. Duties performed in the UK which are other than merely incidental to the duties performed overseas may lead to the income being taxed in the UK unless paid by an overseas employer. If this happens there may be exemption relief by the Double Tax Treaty between the UK and the country in which the individual now lives. Normally, moving expenses, to a maximum of £8000 in total, including temporary subsistence expenses in connection with the move to take up work abroad, will not be liable to UK tax.

Income from investments in the UK remains liable to UK tax, generally by deduction at source. By Inland Revenue concession, bank deposit interest may be paid gross to a 'non-resident' and an individual should advise his bank or building society of his impending 'non-resident' status before departure. The tax credit attributable to dividends may be refunded in part to the 'non-resident' individual where the country in which he is now living has a Double Tax Treaty with the UK. However, this will normally involve such income being taxable in the new country.

To coincide with the introduction of self-assessment new rules apply when someone working abroad rents their home while away. From 6 April 1996 the person paying the rent or the agent acting is responsible to pay each quarter to the Inland Revenue the tax due on the rent unless the Revenue authorise the payments to be made without deduction of tax. In calculating the tax due, letting costs such as interest and repairs may be deducted as expenses of the letting. Prior to the 6 April 1996 the rent was paid direct to the non-resident net of basic rate tax and the non-resident reclaimed the tax back on the expenses. The appointment of a UK agent responsible for paying the tax may simplify the process.

Mortgage interest relief can continue to be claimed by concession when the period of working abroad is not expected to exceed four years. When this concession applies, employees can continue to pay their mortgage under MIRAS arrangements. However as the relief under MIRAS is now given only at 15 per cent, it may be advantageous to claim the relief on the interest paid against the profit on the letting and gain relief at 24 (1996–97) per cent. Similarly when the mortgage exceeds £30,000 it will normally be advantageous to claim the relief on the interest paid against the rent rather than under MIRAS.

British subjects may continue to claim personal allowances while 'non-resident' and this can be advantageous where small amounts of dividend income or rent are involved. In such cases, it is usually advisable to transfer any bank or building society deposits offshore, as the normal concession regarding payment of interest gross is withdrawn.

Capital gains realised while the person is in full-time employment abroad should not be liable to UK tax.

Working abroad while a UK resident

If an employee works outside the UK for more than twelve months but does not cover a tax year the individual remains UK resident. Fortunately, all is not lost provided the absence abroad is for a period of 365 qualifying days since a 100 per cent tax relief is available for related earnings. With this exception, all other income remains liable to UK tax.

The '365 qualifying day' period is calculated as days of absence from the UK (not necessarily working days) together with intervening periods in the UK provided that these UK visits do not exceed: (a) one sixth of the period between the start and end of the qualifying period, and (b) no visit exceeds 62 days. For this purpose it is whether a person is abroad at midnight that determines absence. This difficult rule is best illustrated by an example:

Days of Absence	Days in UK	Total
01.10.94 — 20.12.94		81 days
	21.12.94 — 04.01.95	15 days
05.01.95 — 31.03.95		85 days
	01.04.95 — 15.04.95	15 days
16.04.95 — 15.10.95		183 days
	16.10.95 — 20.12.95	66 days
21.12.95 — 28.02.96		70 days

A 100 per cent deduction would be available against earnings for the period 1 October 1994 to 15 October 1995. However, the Autumn 1995 stay, although less than a sixth of the total period, exceeds 62 days and thus no further relief is available. A return abroad on 15 December 1995 would have enabled 100 per cent tax relief for the whole period. Timing is vital!

Generally, expenses to take up, or return from, overseas employment together with appropriate subsistence and lodging will not be taxable. Where the overseas duties involve a period abroad of over 60 continuous days the payment of travel expenses of spouse and children for up to two visits a year will not be taxed in the UK.

Other considerations

When an individual continues to be employed by his UK employer while abroad he may be able to remain within the employer's pension scheme, depending on length of period. If employed by an overseas employer then appropriate alternative pension arrangements may be required.

A person's National Insurance position depends on whether he continues to be paid from the UK and, if so, where he is working. In the event that no employer or employee contributions are being made, Class 3 voluntary contributions should be considered.

Not all countries have the UK's National Health Service and adequate medical insurance should be arranged to cover illness and, if necessary, repatriation.

Summary

- Business trips abroad, of less than a year, will not change UK tax position of employee who remains liable to UK tax on worldwide income and gains.
- Business trips of over a year but which do not cover a whole tax year (5 April following), will only affect UK tax position if employee is absent for 365 'qualifying' days.
- Long-term business trips, if under full-time employment contract of over a year, will remove a person from UK tax on overseas income and possibly UK source income as well.

15

The Family Home

The family home is the biggest investment that most individuals ever make. There is a common misconception that a family home is a 'tax-free zone' — it is not always the case, as this chapter will explain.

Buying a family home

Interest relief

One of the most important matters for individuals buying their own home is the availability of tax relief on interest payments made on the loan used to buy it. This relief has been slowly eroded by the government in various ways over the years.

There are two areas where interest relief is given on a loan, one where a property is purchased and let commercially, which will be covered in Chapter 16, and the other where the property is the individual's 'only or main residence' (the family home).

In both cases the basic requirement is that the loan must have been used:

- in purchasing the land and/or building (which can include a caravan or house-boat); or
- in improving or developing the land or buildings on the land; or
- in replacing a previously qualifying loan.

As far as the family home is concerned, income tax relief is available on interest payable on a loan up to a maximum of £30,000 at a rate of 15 per cent. This relief is usually given by means of the MIRAS system (Mortgage Interest Relief At Source) where the borrower pays the interest, net of the available relief, to the lender. However, there are certain circumstances where tax relief is available but the MIRAS system cannot apply. In such circumstances relief will be given by means of an adjustment to a coding notice or in tax assessments.

The MIRAS system can only be operated by the lender where confirmation is given by the borrower that he qualifies for relief on the interest. The onus of proof is firmly placed on the borrower. He must therefore notify the lender if he believes that the loan no longer qualifies for relief.

Interest relief may also be available for limited periods on a bridging loan where an individual has a mortgage on one property which is not immediately sold on the move to a new main residence.

In the past it was possible to obtain interest relief on loans for home improvements. Since 6 April 1988, such loans have not been allowable broadly unless the loan was made prior to 6 April 1988 or the property is let commercially.

Difficulties in obtaining relief may occur where individuals have two houses. In those circumstances it is a question of fact as to which is the main residence and therefore which property loan attracts interest relief. It is important to ensure that the loan is in place in respect of the property for which relief will be available.

Another difficulty is where the individual does not live in the family home for part or all of any tax year. In this case, interest paid may not qualify for tax relief. Absences may be unavoidable and there are certain concessionary reliefs given by the Inland Revenue in the following circumstances including:

- Temporary absence up to one year.
- Absence for up to a maximum of four years either in the UK or overseas caused by employment requirements, providing the property was used as the main residence prior to the absence, and it can be reasonably expected that this will be the case upon return.

Interest relief will only be available on a re-mortgage where the new loan replaces an existing loan which currently qualifies for relief. No increase in the loan will be allowable.

Stamp duty

Stamp duty is a tax paid by the purchaser based upon the value of the property he has bought. Since March 1993, stamp duty at a rate of one per cent has been applied to property purchased over £60,000, below this limit no charge is made. Provisions exist to counter the avoidance of stamp duty in respect of certain land transactions. Advice should be sought to ensure that these provisions are not applicable.

Value added tax

Individuals building their own home with the intention of using it as their main residence may be able to reclaim VAT paid on certain materials used in the building.

There are a number of specific requirements including a three month time limit from the date of completion of the property within which to make the claim. Professional advice should be sought.

Life assurance and mortgages

Currently the most common method of mortgage repayment is the low-cost endowment whereby the borrower pays only interest to the lender and a separate premium to the insurance company.

The policy can be transferred from property to property and should provide for the repayment of the loan at the end of the policy term. Depending upon investment returns there may be a surplus although there have recently been reductions in bonus levels.

New style plans offer automatic reviews of investment performance and, given the right investment conditions, unit linked contracts should achieve greater longer term rewards. Nevertheless old style endowment plans can provide good growth prospects, particularly those effected before 14 March 1984 which still attract life assurance premium relief.

Endowment mortgages may not provide sufficient flexibility, security or tax efficiency for some investors who may prefer to consider either pension, PEP or capital and interest mortgages.

A capital and interest mortgage is structured to pay off a loan by the end of the specified period. Normally a mortgage protection plan would be arranged to repay the loan in the event of the death of the borrower, although it may well prove more cost effective to arrange a whole-of-life plan should the borrower intend to move property several times.

Occupying the family home

It may be that rooms in the house are used for either lodgers or for business purposes. In these circumstances, additional income tax relief may be available on either the rent being received from the lodger, or the expenses being borne in relation to a room being used for the business.

Renting

Previously tax was payable on rent received from a lodger after deduction of expenses incurred in providing the room and related services. The government introduced what is now known as 'rent a room' relief for the tax year 1992–93 and subsequent years which operates under the following conditions:

- The room or rooms must be let furnished.
- A maximum figure of £3250 of gross rents receivable is exempt from taxation. Any rents receivable in excess of this figure are charged to tax in full without any deduction for expenses.
- If items are purchased to furnish the accommodation, relief cannot be claimed for the expenditure if the exemption of £3250 is claimed. It may therefore be appropriate to elect for the scheme exemption not to apply in a particular tax year if it is beneficial to claim a deduction for expenses.
- There are two methods of claiming relief for expenses. Under the 'renewals basis', items such as carpets and large pieces of furniture do not qualify as an expense in the year when first purchased. They do however attract capital allowances where the expenditure is written-off over a period of time. Replacement costs, when incurred, qualify for a deduction in later years. Under the alternative basis, the landlord claims a deduction each year for wear and tear on furnishings by using a strict formula. This equates to 10 per cent of the rent receivable, less rates, in each year.
- Any loss will be available to reduce any future rental income from the same property.
- Mortgage interest payments are not considered to be an allowable expense in arriving at the net profit (or loss) on the rents. Tax relief will normally be given on the first £30,000 under MIRAS when the property is the borrower's main residence.
- The election to have 'rent a room' relief must be made and with-

drawn by written notice to the Inspector of Taxes within one year of the end of the tax year.

Business purposes

If part of a property is used for business purposes, then a proportion of the total expenses of the house can be claimed as a deduction against the business profits. The calculation of relief available will depend upon whether a room is used exclusively for business purposes or whether it is only proportionally used. In either case, it will be necessary to agree the amount with the Inland Revenue.

Although significant reliefs can be obtained in relation to both the lodger and the business use of a private residence, the capital gains position on disposal may be adversely affected. This is covered next.

Selling the family home

Capital gains tax

An individual selling a 'dwelling house or part of a dwelling house which has at any time been, during the period of ownership, his only or main residence or land which he has for his own occupation and enjoyment, with that residence as its gardens or grounds up to the permitted area' will be exempt from capital gains tax on the proceeds of the disposal. This is commonly called principal private residence relief and is potentially very valuable.

As with interest relief, absences from the house are disregarded in certain circumstances:

- A period or periods not exceeding three years.
- Any period throughout which the individual was employed outside the UK.
- Any period or periods not exceeding four years throughout which the individual could not reside in the property as a consequence of the situation of his place of work, or conditions imposed by his employer requiring him to reside elsewhere.

In all cases it is essential that after the period of absence actual occupation is resumed.

The relief is also available where an individual has to reside in 'job-related' accommodation but does intend, in due course, to occupy a house that he owns as his main residence.

In certain circumstances the relief can be available on a property occupied by a dependent relative.

The last 36 months of ownership is always regarded as deemed occupation for the principal private residence exemption.

It is therefore likely in the majority of circumstances that an individual's main residence will carry no charge to capital gains tax, provided it has been the main residence throughout ownership. However, there are a number of points to be noted where this is not the case:

- If a property has been partially rented, then the capital gains tax relief will not be available broadly on the area let for the period of the letting. In these circumstances, the gain is proportionally calculated; the gain relating to the rented part may be exempted by up to £40,000.

- Where a room or proportion of a room is used exclusively for business purposes, the gain attributable to that portion will be liable to capital gains tax, without any relief for the principal private residence exemption. To avoid this possible problem never use a room exclusively for business purposes.

- Another area which causes problems is in relation to the sale of land or adjoining buildings attaching to a property where any gain may or may not be exempt by the private residence exemption. The law states that the land which is covered by the exemption is an area (inclusive of the site of the house) of 0.5 of a hectare (slightly more than an acre) or such area, as the appeal commissioners may determine as being necessary for the reasonable enjoyment of the property. It should be noted that land retained after a house sale and subsequently disposed of, whether within the 0.5 hectare or not, is unlikely to be covered by the exemption. This is a complex area where it is essential to take professional advice.

The principal private residence relief is obviously very important to individuals and can be used as often as required during a person's lifetime. Care should be taken where properties are bought, renovated and sold on a regular basis, as the Inland Revenue may argue that a trade is being carried on.

Inheritance tax

Typically, the family home comprises a significant part of an individual's estate. Inheritance tax is levied on estates in excess of £200,000 (1996–97) at a rate of 40 per cent. Given the significance of the family home it is essential that proper attention is given to its form of ownership and how this is to be passed on, during lifetime (see Chapter 19) or on death (see Chapter 21).

When a property is purchased by a couple (usually spouses), it can be legally owned either as 'joint tenants' or 'tenants in common'. In the case of joint tenants, the house is shared and, on the death of either party, will automatically revert to the survivor. Where a house is held as 'tenants in common', each joint owner owns half of the house and it is possible for each of them to transfer their share of the house independently from the other. In the majority of cases, joint ownership will be in the form of joint tenancy but consideration needs to be given to which option is most suitable, especially when valuable property is involved.

Summary

- Interest relief only available on £30,000 borrowings at 15 per cent.
- 'Rent a Room' relief available when letting rooms in main residence.
- Stamp duty of 1 per cent payable on purchase of properties with a value over £60,000.
- Capital gains exemption available on principal private residence. May be restricted in certain circumstances.
- The family home is a substantial asset for inheritance tax purposes. Proper attention should be given to the form of ownership.

16

The Second or Rented Home

It is becoming more common for individuals to own a second home. These properties are generally bought as holiday homes although they are also acquired as investments. Clearly the purchase, retention and ultimate sale of such assets will have taxation consequences which need to be considered at as early a stage as possible. References made below to sales assume that the disposal is charged to capital gains tax. Care should be taken if second homes are bought, refurbished and sold on a regular basis. In this case the Inland Revenue may argue that a trade is being undertaken. If this argument succeeds none of the capital gains tax reliefs and allowances (including principal private residence relief and indexation allowance, referred to below) will be available.

Purchase for own use and investment potential

It was noted in the previous chapter that tax relief at 15 per cent is available for interest on loans of up to £30,000 used to finance the acquisition of the family home. Such interest relief is only available if the borrowings finance the purchase of the individual's only or main residence. It may be that the purchase of the second home will be funded out of borrowed money. Tax relief cannot be obtained in respect of interest on loans to acquire a second home as this would not be accepted as the main residence. There is a possibility that interest relief is obtainable on such a loan if the property is to be rented out; this is considered in more detail later.

When the second home is sold a liability to capital gains tax may arise on any profit. However, the amount of the taxable profit may be reduced by the following:

- If the property was acquired before 31 March 1982, its value at that date can be substituted for the actual cost in calculating the taxable gain. Clearly such a substitution will only be worthwhile if the March 1982 valuation exceeds the actual cost.

- An allowance is given (the indexation allowance) to reflect the rise in the Retail Prices Index from the date of acquisition, or 31 March 1982 if later, to the date of disposal. Currently this allowance represents approximately 85 per cent of the cost or March 1982 value when taken from 31 March 1982 to date.

The previous chapter considered how the principal private residence relief can eliminate any capital gains tax on the disposal of the family home. Where an individual owns two or more homes it is possible to effectively choose which one of them should be the 'principal private residence' for these purposes. The individual must notify the Tax Office in writing of this choice within two years of the acquisition of the second home. Whether such an election to treat the second home as the principal private residence is beneficial will depend on a number of factors including the periods of occupation (both deemed and actual) and the amount of potential profit in each property. It should also be noted that, once the second home is chosen as the principal residence for a period, the family home by definition ceases to be so for capital gains tax purposes. As a result, although tax can be saved on the disposal of the second home, a liability can occur when the family home is sold. With careful planning it may be possible to limit the amount of tax payable on disposal of the second home.

It is interesting to compare the capital gains tax and income tax position of the second home. Although the second home can be 'chosen' as the principal residence for capital gains tax purposes, for income tax interest relief purposes the determination of the main residence is purely one of fact.

If the second home is not sold but is kept until death, it will form part of the individual's estate for inheritance tax purposes. No reliefs are available to reduce the value of the property on which inheritance tax will be charged. However, no capital gains tax arises on death and a tax-free uplift to its then market value occurs.

Letting the property

The potential additional financing cost of acquiring a second home often means that the property is rented out so that the rental income contributes towards or covers the interest payments and upkeep. The rents received will represent a taxable source of income.

For 1996–97 tax on property income will be collected as part of the interim payment on 31 January 1997. This will be based on the previous year's figure and any balance due once the actual details are known will be payable on 31 January 1998.

For 1997–98 onwards the tax will be payable as part of the interim payments on 31 January in the year of assessment and 31 July following (based on the previous year's income figure) with any balance being paid on the following 31 January.

Furnished and unfurnished accommodation

Since 6 April 1995, all income from property in the UK, let furnished or unfurnished, is taxed under new Schedule A rules. Although the income from such property is taxed as investment income, it is calculated as if the activity of letting the property is a trade and ordinary accounting principles will apply.

Under the rules which prevailed prior to 6 April 1995, different types of letting had to be kept separate and there were restrictions in setting a loss on one type of lease against a profit on another. Since that date, losses brought forward on any lease are available to be set off against profits made on any letting of property in the UK and the income from such property is pooled for this purpose.

Capital allowances may be claimed on equipment used in the management of the property as a deduction from the Schedule A rent. It is not possible to claim capital allowances on furniture and equipment used in living accommodation. However, a 'wear and tear' allowance of 10 per cent of the gross rents less rates is available in respect of income from furnished property.

Interest payable in respect of property lettings will be allowable as a deduction in computing the taxable income. In the same way, other related expenses may be deducted from the rental income such as insurance, repairs, rates, lighting of common areas and bad debts.

The disposal of either furnished or unfurnished property may result in a capital gains tax liability by reference to cost or value at 31 March 1982 and any indexation allowance available. It will be necessary to consider whether the property has been the principal private residence of the owner and whether the letting exemption referred to in the previous chapter is available.

The property will be a chargeable asset for inheritance tax purposes and, as with the family home, no reliefs are available to reduce the chargeable value.

Holiday accommodation

For tax purposes the letting of furnished holiday premises is regarded as a trade. It has, in the past, been taxed under Schedule D Case VI but, with effect from 6 April 1995, it will be treated as Schedule A income. The rules and changes outlined in the section above will therefore also apply to furnished holiday letting. In addition, the points below continue to apply.

For tax purposes, holiday accommodation is any property which in a 12 month period:

- is *available* for commercial letting to the public as holiday accommodation for at least 140 days;
- is *actually* let for at least 70 days; and
- for a seven month period, which need not be continuous, is not let to the same person for more than 31 days continuously.

Class 4 and possibly Class 2 National Insurance contributions will be payable on income from furnished holiday lettings. Expenses are deductible from the rents following ordinary accounting principles and losses are available against other income. Capital allowances may be available on relevant expenditure and the net earnings after capital allowances are relevant earnings for the purposes of personal pensions or retirement annuities.

The renting of furnished holiday accommodation can have VAT consequences. If the total of rents receivable exceeds the VAT registration limit, £47,000 per annum from 29 November 1995, then registration will be required.

Although when the property is sold a liability to capital gains tax may arise, the amount of that liability can be reduced or the payment of the tax can be deferred by virtue of certain reliefs.

If the sale of the property takes place once the individual is over 50 years old, retirement relief may be available.

The taxpayer may also be able to take advantage of the 'roll-over' relief provisions. If on disposal of the property the sale proceeds are reinvested in certain qualifying assets within one year before and three years after the date of disposal, the gain arising can effectively be deferred until the 'new' asset is sold.

The property might also be eligible for capital gains tax gift relief. This would enable the taxpayer to gift the asset without any immediate capital gains tax consequences. The tax arising on the gift would be deferred until the asset was sold by the person who acquired it.

For inheritance tax purposes, although the property would fall into the individual's estate and be theoretically chargeable, the total value of the property might be eligible to be reduced by business property relief. The property would, therefore, escape the charge to inheritance tax.

Overseas property

If a holiday home is purchased overseas and rented out the income remains chargeable to UK income tax. From 6 April 1995 interest paid on a loan taken out to purchase a property overseas will be allowable against rental income arising on the property. If an overseas property is to be acquired local advice should be taken as soon as possible to ensure that all local tax and legal issues are thoroughly considered and understood.

General

Capital gains tax reinvestment relief is available in respect of all gains made by individuals. This depends on the reinvestment of the gain into qualifying shares, within the conditions laid down for the relief. Professional advice should be sought.

Summary

- Interest relief only available on second home if rented out.
- Capital gains tax payable on disposal of second home subject to availability of reinvestment or other reliefs.
- Election available to treat second home as principal residence for capital gains tax purposes.
- Second home is a chargeable asset for inheritance tax purposes.
- Potentially significant tax advantages to letting of furnished holiday accommodation.
- If letting overseas property, beware local taxes and regulations.

17

Tax and Offshore Investments

It is commonly thought that one way of avoiding tax on investments is to invest outside the UK. Unfortunately this is generally incorrect as the majority of people living in the UK are taxed on their worldwide income whether or not it is brought into the country. However, offshore investments can have a part to play in reducing exposure to tax in appropriate circumstances. This can be particularly useful in certain situations for individuals born abroad or whose father was born abroad. Separate advice should be taken.

This chapter considers the main types of offshore investments. Generally it is only investments based in countries with low tax rates, the most common of which are Bermuda, Luxembourg, the Channel Islands and the Isle of Man, which are attractive to the investor.

Offshore deposit accounts

All the major UK banks and building societies have representative offices overseas, particularly the Channel Islands and the Isle of Man, and they all cater in some way for the UK investor. The rates of interest paid on the accounts is similar to those paid within the UK but the essential difference is that interest on the overseas account can be paid without deduction of tax; a UK account can only pay interest gross if a declaration has been made that the investor does not pay tax. However, even though the interest is paid gross it must be declared to the Tax Office. Any tax due will usually be assessed on the interest arising and not the amount brought into the country.

Before investing in offshore deposits of this type, it is important to establish the extent to which the UK bank or building society takes responsibility for the activities of its overseas branch. Consideration should also be given to the level of investor protection offered in the offshore location. Within the UK, deposits with banks are insured so that a compensation fund covers 75 per cent of the first £20,000 of a deposit for each individual. Building society deposits are similarly insured to the extent of 90 per cent of the first £20,000 of a deposit for each individual. The level of depositor protection for investments in the Isle of Man is similar to that provided for bank accounts in the UK but there is no depositor protection scheme in the Channel Islands and Gibraltar.

Offshore funds

The expression 'offshore fund' is a general one which is applied to any investment fund based abroad. Such funds are similar to UK unit trusts but they offer a greater level of freedom in investment than their UK equivalent. They cover a wide range of investments from cash deposits to investments in futures and options. Unlike UK unit trusts, they can be set up to invest either in one or many currencies. The funds can distribute their income to investors gross but as with deposits this income normally has to be declared by the UK investor to the Tax Office. It is also important to note that the funds themselves do not necessarily accumulate tax-free income because if they in turn invest in other countries where tax is deducted at source, that tax cannot be recovered.

There are essentially two main types of funds:

- *Distributor funds:* these funds distribute at least 85 per cent of their received income; if their income is very low (say 1 per cent of the capital value) they will still be eligible for distributor status even if they have not made the required level of distribution.
- *Non-distributor funds*: these funds distribute less than 85 per cent of their received income.

There are important differences in the way these two types of fund are taxed. The income distributed by distributor funds is taxed under Schedule D Case V (see Chapter 1) but provided the fund itself has distributor status, any capital growth which it achieves will have the advantage of being subject to capital gains tax. Conversely all the income from non-distributor funds (sometimes called roll-up funds) is taxed under Schedule D Case VI (see Chapter 1). Furthermore any capital growth is also taxed as income and not as a capital gain, but not until the capital growth is realised.

Distributor funds will often be more attractive because the annual capital gains tax exemption will be available, as will the indexation allowance.

The investments offered by authorised UK unit trusts and investment trusts will provide appropriate investment opportunities for most UK investors.

Despite the capital gains tax disadvantages, the non-distributor fund can have certain attractions to the UK investor, particularly where none of the income whatsoever is distributed. The use of such funds makes it possible to defer the tax on income arising until a later period. Some examples of when this can be used to good effect are as follows.

For individuals remaining within the UK

- *Those coming up to retirement:* individuals may pay higher rate tax while in employment but after retirement their tax rate may go down to the basic rate. By using these investments it is possible to defer the charge to income tax on such investments until the investor's tax rates have reduced.
- *Infant children:* generally the income of infant children arising from parental gifts continues to be taxed as the parent's income. By investing the money into an offshore roll-up fund and only realising that investment once the child has reached the age of 18 the tax charge can be delayed until the child is entitled to use his or her own tax allowances.
- *Non-working spouses:* they may receive variable amounts of investment income and roll-up funds can be used to enable the realisation of just sufficient taxable income to absorb their remaining unused personal tax allowances or lower rate tax band.

UK residents going overseas

Where parents and their infant children expect to live overseas until they achieve non-resident status, an investment in a roll-up fund can enable the income to accumulate. The investment can then be realised and UK income tax avoided on the whole gain. It is necessary to have regard to any tax liability which may arise in the new country of residence.

Offshore insurance bonds

These have certain similarities to offshore funds but are set up as single premium life assurance policies. They have traditionally been marketed by overseas branches of insurance companies to people living abroad, including UK expatriates. The benefits are that investment income and capital growth generally accrue free of tax in the hands of the insurance company, which is usually located in a low-tax country. When the policyholder returns to the UK the investment can be encashed in stages by making use of the 5 per cent part surrender rule (see Chapter 8) or in full in the knowledge that only higher rate but not basic rate income tax will be suffered on the growth achieved.

Such investments have grown in popularity and become more sophisticated in concept. An investor can choose to invest in individual securities rather than in a pooled investment and still shelter the income and capital gains tax arising from the disposals by keeping the ownership within the offshore life assurance company. Investment houses in the Isle of Man and the Channel Islands extend their marketing activities and promote their products directly to UK investors as well as the more usual expatriates. This led the Inland Revenue to attack some of these arrangements in 1990. However, the attack was usually against those investments of a 'highly personalised' nature such as those which invest in securities chosen by the individual. The Inland Revenue have indicated that they will not attack investments where the investor has no investment control over the funds and thus the pooled investment funds of insurance companies are still acceptable.

The UK investor therefore can use this pooled type of fund to defer tax on the actual gains made by the fund while still being able to enjoy tax-free withdrawals of up to 5 per cent of the initial amount invested. Where the UK investor continues to live in this country the total gain on the bond's eventual encashment will be taxed at both basic and higher tax rates depending on circumstances at that time. If the investor is no longer resident on encashment then the UK liability can be avoided completely.

It should be noted that there is expected to be a major reform to the way in which single premium insurance bonds are taxed which may reduce the current tax efficiency of the structure of both UK and offshore investments.

Investor protection

Some offshore investments are covered by the compensation schemes which apply to similar UK equity-based investments. However, many are not and there is not always a comparable form of investor protection available locally.

Some cautionary points

- Some offshore centres do not recognise UK probate (see Chapter 21). Therefore if an individual has made an investment offshore and dies while holding that investment, it may be necessary for probate to be obtained in that location as well as in the UK before the funds can be released. This can be an expensive exercise. The Guernsey authorities recognise UK probate and therefore no separate probate is required for investments in Guernsey. By contrast, separate probate would be required for investments held in Jersey.
- The investor should pay particular attention to the quality of investor protection available in the offshore location.
- The possibilities of using offshore investments to defer tax charges until a later date have been explained. However the rates of tax in the UK at present are relatively low and there is always a danger that the tax charge might be deferred to a period when tax rates are higher.
- Investors would be ill-advised to make offshore investments purely to avoid tax. They should choose the type of investment required and then discover if an advantage is obtainable by placing the investment overseas.

Summary

- Do not invest offshore purely for tax reasons.
- Understand clearly the limits on investor protection.
- Offshore investments can be attractive in particular circumstances, but do not go ahead without considering the risks.

18

Tax and Giving to Charity

This chapter summarises the taxation implications of gifts to charities. Not all forms of charitable giving attract tax benefits. Non tax-efficient examples include flag days and sponsored activities.

In recent years, the government has done much to encourage charitable giving and there are now a number of ways in which donations can be made to benefit both the donor and the charity. These are described below.

Deeds of covenant

A deed of covenant is a legal document. Most charities will be able to assist or supply a standard deed of covenant format. The main features are:

- It is a legal agreement between the charity and the donor for payment to be made each year for a period capable of exceeding three years.
- No goods or services should be received by the donor as a result of payments under the deed.
- The frequency and amount of the payment will be defined within the deed. There is no minimum payment and the frequency of payment can be at any interval. The deed needs to provide for a payment to be made each year that the deed is in force.
- If payment is made before the deed is completed and witnessed it will be ineffective for tax purposes.
- Payments are made net of basic rate tax and the charity is able to reclaim the tax so deducted, thereby increasing the total amount it receives. The tax position of basic rate taxpayers is unaffected by these arrangements. Higher rate taxpayers will be entitled to additional tax relief equivalent to 20 per cent of the covenanted

payment. Non-taxpayers will be required to pay the basic rate tax over to the Inland Revenue.

- The donor needs to provide the charity with a completed certificate R185(AP) which includes full details of the payment in order for the charity to reclaim the income tax deducted by the donor. These certificates are often completed by the charity for signature by the donor. In certain circumstances the charity is able to operate a simplified procedure which avoids the need for a R185(AP) to be completed each year.

When charitable gifts are intended on an annual basis, although not to the same charity, the covenant could be made through the Charities Aid Foundation (CAF). The CAF is itself a charity whose purpose is to improve the quality and amount of charitable giving. Their address is 48 Pembury Road, Tonbridge, Kent. The CAF will operate an account and allow the donor to direct the covenanted payments (with the tax relief) to the nominated charities. A small charge is made for this service, which is usually deducted from the covenanted payment.

If it is intended to make a one-off gift it is possible to use a Deposited Covenant Scheme. This scheme works by the individual loaning the charity the amount of money he wishes to gift, and then entering into a covenant with the charity. The monies loaned to the charity are repaid on an annual basis to pay the instalments due under the deed.

It is also possible in certain circumstances to pay the membership subscription of a charitable organisation by a deed of covenant. The individual covenants to pay his membership subscription to the charity for as long as he remains a member of the charity, which allows the member to resign at any time and so terminate the covenant. There are some restrictions on such arrangements. In particular, they are ineffective for tax purposes where the member receives any benefit in return for his subscription, unless the charity's sole or main purpose is either the preservation of property for the public benefit or the conservation of wildlife for the public benefit, for example, The National Trust, English Heritage, RSPB and the RSPCA.

Gift Aid

Gift Aid was introduced for gifts made on or after 1 October 1990. The main features are as follows:

- Income tax relief at basic rate and higher rate is available to individuals for cash gifts made under the scheme. The amount received by the charity is treated as being net of basic rate tax which can be reclaimed in the same way as with deeds of covenant.

- The payment (after deduction of basic rate tax) must be at least £250 and must not exceed the taxable income of the donor.
- Gifts which have already qualified for an existing income tax relief, for example, as a payment under a deed of covenant, will be ineligible, as will charitable bequests made on the donor's death.
- The gift must not be used by the charity to acquire property from the donor or any person connected with him.
- The donor or any person connected with him must not receive any benefit from the charity as a result of making the gift. (There is however a threshold below which benefits can be ignored, the level being 2.5 per cent of the amount of the gift or £250 whichever is the less).

Gift Aid is extremely simple with few formalities. The gift needs to be certified so that the charity can reclaim tax from the Inland Revenue. This is done by completing the appropriate form R190(SD) and sending it to the charity to reclaim the tax. The charity will often provide the completed form for signature by the donor.

A gift to the CAF could be used to obtain the Gift Aid tax benefits where individual gifts of less than £250 but more than that in total are considered. They operate a similar scheme for Gift Aid as the one they have for deeds of covenant.

Payroll Giving

Payroll Giving was introduced in 1986. From 6 April 1996 the amount that can be given under the scheme is £1200 per annum. The main features of the scheme are:

- The employer must operate a scheme approved by the Inland Revenue.
- Under the scheme the employer deducts donations as requested by the employee. The donations qualify for tax relief.
- The employer pays the donations over to an agency charity which acts as a 'clearing house' distributing the payments to the charity/charities nominated by the employee.
- Payments must not qualify for any other income tax relief, for example, as a payment under a deed of covenant.

Payroll giving can only be used with the cooperation of the employer. The employee receives tax relief through the Pay As You Earn system, and the charities receive the money gross from the agency charity.

Bequests under wills

Broadly speaking, charitable bequests are deductible for inheritance tax without limit. As with deeds of covenant, most charities will offer assistance in making charitable bequests in wills. Careful will drafting is required to ensure that the benefits to the charity and the deceased's estate are maximised. This is a complex area where professional advice should be sought.

Summary

- Tax-efficient gifts to charity can reduce an individual's tax liability.
- The value of a tax efficient gift to a charity is one-third more than a simple cash donation.
- For gifts of, or totalling more than, £250, Gift Aid is a relatively simple method of making tax efficient gifts to charity.
- Charities offer help and advice to individuals wishing to make tax-efficient gifts.

19

Lifetime Estate Planning

Inheritance tax is primarily a tax relating to death. Inheritance tax becomes payable if the total assets held on death plus any lifetime transfers made within seven years of death exceed the inheritance tax threshold (£200,000 for 1996–97). The excess is taxed at 40 per cent. The tax can also apply at reduced rates to some lifetime gifts at the time they are made.

Satisfactory planning to avoid inheritance tax can sometimes be carried out by Will or even after death, by the family rearranging matters within two years of the death (see Chapter 21). The alternative which many people prefer is to arrange property in their lifetime so that it does not fall within the tax charge.

Although lifetime giving appears to be an obvious way of decreasing a future inheritance tax bill, it should not be undertaken lightly. Special care must be taken to retain sufficient income and capital to provide for future maintenance in any circumstances — for example, nursing care might be required. In addition, although some actions can give an inheritance tax advantage, there may be other tax disadvantages. The capital gains tax effect in particular must be considered.

Any gift of specific assets (or a sale of such assets in order to give cash) will also be a capital gains tax disposal. Care must be taken where such assets have increased in value that an immediate capital gains tax charge does not result. It is possible in some cases and particularly with gifts of business assets to 'hold over' the gain, that is, pass the gain on to the recipient of the gift rather than face a present tax bill. For stamp duty, outright gifts have exemption.

Potentially exempt transfers

The most straightforward method of lifetime tax planning is to make absolute gifts to individual beneficiaries. Since 1986 it has been possible to make a potentially exempt transfer (PET) of any amount to another individual without giving rise to any inheritance tax charges at the time of gift. If the person making the gift then survives for seven years after the gift the transfer will be completely exempt for inheritance tax purposes. If survival for seven years is not achieved the transfer will come into the reckoning at the date of death. Such lifetime transfers will not actually give rise to a tax charge unless in total they exceed the inheritance tax threshold. Even if there is a tax charge, it (but not the value of the gift) can be reduced by as much as 80 per cent depending on the time between the gift and the death. The possibility that the person making the gift may die within seven years creating a tax liability can be eased by taking out a short-term life insurance policy to cover the position. The combination of a PET and an insurance policy is a fairly effective and straightforward way of reducing inheritance tax and giving peace of mind.

It is not possible or desirable for all persons to make large PETs absolutely to beneficiaries. For one thing the intended beneficiary may be too young — say grandchildren — to receive a large gift or it may not be obvious which of several beneficiaries should benefit, in order to take over the family business, for example. Some of these points can be solved by using trusts (see Chapter 20) but for many the real concern will be more practical; the assets themselves will be required to produce income or other benefits for the person who would otherwise have made the gift.

Reservation of benefit

Until 1986 it was possible to make a gift of an asset (for example, a house) but retain some benefit from it (living in it) without that asset becoming taxable on a later death. In 1986, parallel to the PET, the reservation of benefit (ROB) concept was introduced. The main feature of ROB is that a gift made after 1986 will be taxable to inheritance tax on a later death if the person making the gift has received some benefit from the item given away. This rule applies even if the gift was a PET and the seven years have already passed. The benefit does not have to be a continuous one and will count unless incidental (for example, giving the house to your daughter and then later making social visits on family occasions). The benefit rule is also suspended in some cases where the person making the gift has *later* become incapable of looking after him or herself and is receiving a benefit by being looked after in the house, which was given away. These exceptions and others covered later should not be relied upon without seeking further advice. The safest rule to adopt is that no benefit should be taken from any property which has been given away.

Exemptions

There are many exemptions and reliefs which can apply to inheritance tax. The main ones for use with lifetime giving in most normal circumstances are:

Spouse exemption: an unlimited amount can be given by one spouse to another.

Annual exemption: up to £3000 per annum can be given in total. If no gifts were made in the previous tax year that £3000 can also be used. Exemptions from other previous years cannot be used.

Small gifts: up to £250 in total can be given to any person in any one tax year provided no other gifts have been made. There is no limit to the number of donees.

Regular gifts: regular gifts made as part of income expenditure can be exempt. The payment of reasonable premiums on a life insurance policy for the benefit of the donee is an example. This exemption can be particularly useful.

Charitable gifts: outright gifts to UK charities are exempt.

Gifts to political parties: outright gifts are exempt without limit.

Gifts on marriage: a parent can give £5000 to a child on the marriage of that child. A grandparent can give £2500 and others £1000.

Gifts of business or agricultural property: these can qualify for special reliefs of up to 100 per cent. Various conditions must be satisfied. If death occurs within seven years further conditions must also be satisfied.

The exemptions outlined above can be used to make modest gifts and this might be quite sufficient for many people. If an exempt gift or PET is made it is not necessary to inform the Inland Revenue of the gift at the time it is made. This will be picked up by the Inland Revenue on the death of the person making the gift, so it is useful to make a note of gifts as and when they are made.

Business assets

Business assets (for example, private company shares) are particularly useful for gifting during lifetime. Not only is relief for business assets likely if the company is trading but the gift can often be made without ROB problems, where the gift is made via a trust, even though the person making the gift remains a director, continues to take a reasonable income as a director and might still control voting rights. The donor will not be able to enjoy any dividends from the gifted shares but many private companies pay very low dividends or none at all so it may not be much of a disadvantage.

The capital gains tax position is also favourable. If the person making the gift of business assets is aged 50 or more then retirement relief may be available. Even if not, the gain can normally be held over with no immediate tax charge.

Care must be taken to plan adequately for retirement through pension provision (see Chapter 12). If no provision is made the business may need to be sold to produce adequate funds. In such a case the business assets will not be there to gift.

Chargeable transfers

Not all gifts will be exempt, or PETs. Some lifetime transfers could be chargeable to inheritance tax when made. The main examples of chargeable lifetime transfers are gifts to a discretionary trust (see Chapter 20) and gifts to or from certain companies. If a lifetime gift is chargeable it will be charged to tax at one half of the death rates (20 per cent instead of 40 per cent) after the threshold of £200,000 (for 1996–97 onwards) has been exceeded. For most transferors chargeable transfers need not be a concern.

Planning points

For many people their home is their main asset. Other assets such as cash or stocks and shares will often be needed to produce income for normal living requirements. This leaves relatively little scope for making lifetime gifts which will be effective. A gift of the house for example would be caught by the ROB provisions mentioned earlier. What can be done in such circumstances?

The following are examples of possible planning points. In all cases it would be advisable to seek professional guidance.

House

Great consideration must be given before any action is taken with the home. This is obviously needed for living in and could easily involve ROB problems if given away. Occupation must be assured for the owner and any surviving spouse. It is however possible to gain an inheritance tax advantage by:

- Giving away a share of the house to someone who will also live there with each joint owner paying their share of outgoings.
- Giving away the house and paying a full commercial rent for any future occupation.
- Disposing of a future interest in the house while retaining present occupation. Careful consideration needs to be paid to the capital gains tax aspect of this, particularly if the house is likely to be sold after occupation ceases.

Other assets

- Can be converted into an annuity to maintain income and release surplus capital for gifts.
- Surplus income or capital can be used to fund a life policy in the name of a beneficiary. On the death of the person taking out the policy the beneficiary will receive the proceeds tax-free.
- In husband and wife cases the policy can be framed so that the proceeds are paid out only on the death of the last survivor. This can then be used to assist in payment of the inheritance tax likely to be due on the second death if the spouse exemption is applied on the first death.
- Can be used to purchase a bond giving separate income and capital rights with income rights being retained. Many insurance companies offer schemes along these lines but care is needed to choose one which is both effective for inheritance tax and also has a low risk of attack by the Inland Revenue.
- Invest in assets which can give relief from inheritance tax, for example, business assets, agricultural property, woodlands.

Summary

- Care is needed to safeguard income before considering making lifetime gifts.
- PETs can be effective where appropriate in mitigating inheritance tax.
- No benefit should be retained or taken from any property given away.
- Use exemptions wisely.
- Business assets can be useful for lifetime giving.
- The home can be used to mitigate inheritance tax but great care is needed.
- Insurance policies or other products can play a role in tax mitigation.
- Investing in assets which qualify for reliefs from inheritance tax can reduce the tax bill while not necessarily reducing income or capital.

20

Saving Tax and Worries Through Trusts

To many people, the word 'Trust' means something close to the black arts. This chapter strips away the mystique, deals with some basic principles and looks briefly at some of the tax aspects of the most common forms of trusts.

Trusts developed in the Middle Ages at the time of the Crusades to safeguard lands and other assets. Today they provide very flexible arrangements that are used for a wide variety of purposes. Consider first a few basic definitions.

What is a trust?

A trust is the relationship between three 'parties'. The first is the *settlor* who gives or settles assets on *trustees*, who are the second party. The trustees own the assets and administer them as set out in the trust deed. The trustees hold the assets on behalf of the *beneficiaries* (the third party) who have an interest in the trust assets which will be set out in the trust document. This is known as the trust deed.

Types of private trust

The four main types of private trust are:

Life interest trusts

In this kind of trust, otherwise described as an interest in possession trust, the beneficiary entitled to the income is known as the 'life tenant' (or 'liferenter' in Scotland). The assets may be held ultimately for different beneficiaries who are known as the 'remaindermen' (or 'fee' in Scotland). The trustees could own a house, for example, in which the beneficiary is allowed to live rent free.

Discretionary trusts

These are a most flexible form of trust where the trustees have broad powers to retain income in the trust for up to 21 years or to make payments out of income or capital at their discretion to any one or more of a group of beneficiaries named in the trust deed.

Accumulation and maintenance trusts

Accumulation and maintenance trusts are a special type of discretionary trust with favourable inheritance tax rules. These trusts are usually intended to benefit children and grandchildren, and at least one beneficiary must be entitled either to income or to receive capital by the age of 25 years. The idea of these settlements is that the trustees accumulate income and are allowed to apply it for the education, maintenance or benefit of any of the beneficiaries. Income which is not paid out is held in the trust, but this can only be done for up to 21 years.

Bare trusts

In these cases the trustees hold the assets in name only and are usually referred to as 'nominees'. The beneficiaries actually own the assets and could ask for them to be transferred into their own names. For tax purposes the income and capital gains of a bare trust belong to the beneficiary and not to the trust.

Taxation of trusts

This is a complex area where professional specialist advice is essential.

Income tax

Trustees of all trusts are required to deal with the payment of basic rate tax liability on all income together with additional rate liability on accumulation and maintenance and discretionary trusts.

Capital gains tax

Assets put into and taken out of trusts can result in capital gains tax. Gains on transfers to discretionary settlements are entitled to hold over relief but relief for gains on transfers to other types of trust depend upon special business property qualifications.

Trustees pay capital gains tax in the usual way and have annual exemptions available to them. Life interest trusts pay tax at 24 per cent, accumulation and maintenance and discretionary trusts at 34 per cent (1996–97).

Inheritance tax

Assets put into life interest and accumulation and maintenance trusts will usually be potentially exempt transfers (PETs). A transfer to a discretionary trust will be a chargeable transfer. Inheritance tax charges can arise on transfers out of a discretionary trust but not in the case of an accumulation and maintenance trust.

The assets of a life interest trust are regarded as belonging to the beneficiary who is described as having an 'interest in possession'.

Discretionary trusts are subject to a special tax regime which levies a small inheritance tax charge every ten years.

Settlors benefiting from the trust

The settlor must not be capable of getting a benefit from trust assets. Otherwise the trust may not be tax effective, and tax advantages will be lost. The deed should include a 'long stop' beneficiary (normally a charity) so that in case all the named beneficiaries die the property cannot be returned, or treated as returned, for tax purposes, to the settlor.

Settlements on children

There are rules to deny tax advantages where parents set up trusts in favour of their children who are under the age of 18 and unmarried, subject to a de minimis limit of £100 of income (and in some cases capital) per tax year.

Uses of trusts

Inheritance tax

Trusts can be very useful for inheritance tax planning where the settlor wishes to reduce the value of his estate but keep control over the trust assets by being a trustee. This would be in preference to making an outright gift.

Capital gains tax

Trusts can help reduce capital gains tax liabilities. Although the annual capital gains exemption is half that of an individual, all trusts have a lower rate of capital gains tax than that of the top marginal rate applicable to individuals.

Death in service benefits/life insurance

It is usually a good idea to have policies put in trust so that on death the proceeds of the policy are paid outside the individual's estate for inheritance tax purposes. This is an easy procedure to adopt. It may take some months to obtain a grant of probate and dependants may require cash in the meantime. By having a policy in this way the proceeds can be paid out quickly with the minimum of formality.

Other

Finally, trusts need not be used for tax advantages alone. They can be effective for providing finance for the younger 'spendthrift' generation, for day-to-day matters, without giving the ability to squander the underlying capital. Trusts can also be used to enable someone to give assets away but still control their destiny by acting as a trustee. When formed early enough trusts can also be effectively used to put assets beyond the reach of creditors in the event of bankruptcy or out of the reach of former spouses in the event of divorce.

Summary

Consider the use of trusts:

- To protect wealth.
- To save inheritance tax.
- To save capital gains tax.
- For control over capital while providing income to beneficiaries.

21
Death

There are a number of legal, administrative and tax aspects relating to the death of an individual. The rules vary depending on where in the UK the deceased was domiciled.

The estate

The assets owned by an individual at the time of his death are known as his free estate.

The will

An individual's estate will be administered after the date of his death by his executors if he has made a will or by his administrators if he has not. If an individual dies in England and Wales without making a will, then he dies intestate and his estate will be administered and distributed in accordance with the Administration of Estates Act 1925. The current rules are set out in Appendix E. The intestacy rules in Scotland are different and are set out in Appendix F.

It is highly desirable to make a will. In this way, an individual (the testator) will die knowing that he has appointed executors who will accept the duty of administering his estate in accordance with his wishes.

Clearly, it is important that an individual's will is kept up to date as circumstances change during life. Family circumstances in particular may change, there may be a need to provide for children and grandchildren in due course. In addition, the family business may become extremely valuable, or property may be sold which had previously been left, in a will that had been drafted some years ago.

A will is revoked by marriage (unless the will states that it was made in contemplation of marriage) and by divorce.

It is for these reasons that an individual should make a will and review it periodically to ensure that it is up to date and reflects current wishes, quite apart from any tax considerations.

The will must be signed by the testator in the presence of two witnesses. The witnesses are required to witness the signing of the will but they are not required to be aware of its contents. If there are any written amendments to the will, they should be initialled by the testator and both witnesses. Nothing should be clipped to the will. Gifts to a witness or spouse of a witness are invalid.

Obtaining probate

On the death of an individual, the executors must value the estate for probate purposes. They might need assistance in this if the property needs to be valued by a specialist valuer. The executors will then complete an application for a Grant of Probate which details the assets and the liabilities that were due at the date of the individual's death. In Scotland, this process is known as obtaining confirmation. The executors or personal representatives may wish to carry out the administration of a simple estate themselves, but can decide to employ the services of an accountant or solicitor to help them in more complicated cases. In addition, the executors must calculate the inheritance tax which is due. In doing this they must include any potentially exempt transfers (PETs) which the person has made within the last seven years, together with any property that must be added to the deceased's free estate.

Such property would include the capital value of the deceased's share in interest in possession trusts (see Chapter 20) and any property previously given away but which is caught by the reservation of benefit rules (see Chapter 19).

The value of the estate which is chargeable to inheritance tax is the net value of the estate after deduction of liabilities due at the date of death of the deceased person, less the nil rate band (or any amount remaining after taking lifetime transfers which have become chargeable into account), less exempt transfers which the deceased person made in his will together with any reliefs that are available.

The main exempt transfers to consider are transfers between spouses. If an individual leaves his entire estate to his spouse or leaves a life interest in the estate to a spouse, then that transfer is totally free from inheritance tax under normal circumstances. Certain other gifts are also exempt including bequests to charities and certain political parties.

The application for the Grant of Probate must be sent to the probate registry, together with the original of the will and a certified copy of the death certificate. (In Scotland application is to the Sheriff Court.) The executors will then need to go for an interview and will need to pay the court fees and any inheritance tax which may be due.

It is normal for the executors to borrow the money to pay the inheritance tax. It is important that the executors take out a loan and not an overdraft because the interest on the loan is allowable for tax purposes, whereas interest on an overdraft is not.

The court will then issue the Grant of Probate, which gives the executors all the authority they need to administer the estate of the individual.

In many cases, a solicitor will be able to obtain probate on behalf of the executors and save them the trouble and inconvenience of a meeting at the probate office.

Sales after death

If land is sold within four years of death for less than probate value, it is possible to substitute the sales proceeds for probate value for inheritance tax purposes. A similar claim may be made for quoted shares within 12 months of death.

Deeds of variation or family arrangement

It is possible to modify the will of a deceased individual within a two-year period following the date of death. The variation can only be made if all affected beneficiaries agree, and that the entitlement of any children under the age of 18 is not decreased following the effects of the deed of variation.

Thus, if someone has made a will and it is found to be tax inefficient, it is possible to rewrite the will, even if only for the purposes of saving inheritance tax.

Rewriting the will has a number of different tax effects. If formal elections are submitted to the Inland Revenue within six months of the date of the document (the deed), then no capital gains tax or inheritance tax implications arise on the changes. In effect, the amendments are treated as having taken place at the date of death.

For income tax purposes the position is different. Income received will be taxed in accordance with the will until the date of the deed of variation. Thereafter income received will be charged to income tax in accordance with the deed of variation.

Other reliefs and exemptions

There are many other reliefs and exemptions not already mentioned such as agricultural property relief, heritage property relief and woodlands relief for example, which may be available.

Husband and wife

Inheritance tax can be avoided completely on the death of the first spouse by simply leaving the residue of the estate to the surviving spouse. However, this may cause a problem on the death of the second spouse, whose own estate now includes the estate of the first spouse. One way around this is to make maximum use of the first spouse's nil rate band on death, possibly through a special form of will trust. Another alternative is to make use of business property relief, where applicable.

Capital gains tax

There is normally no capital gains tax payable on the death of an individual. On someone's death all assets are revalued to market value at the date of death and are then acquired by the legatee at probate value for future capital gains tax purposes.

Taxation of the estate

Executors pay income tax at the basic rate on all income that the estate receives gross. The executors do not receive any personal allowances for income tax, nor do they receive any relief for expenses other than on loan interest on money borrowed to pay the inheritance tax due. The executors are subject to capital gains tax on assets in the estate that they sell, and receive an annual exemption equal to the individual's annual exemption in the year of death and the two succeeding years.

Administration of the estate

Where the administration of the estate takes longer than a year the executors will normally pay statutory interest (currently 6 per cent) on delayed payments to beneficiaries under the will. Thus, if the executors have not paid a gift (a legacy or a bequest) to a beneficiary (the legatee) then they will pay interest at the statutory rate on the value of the bequest. A specific bequest of an asset usually carries a right to the income of the asset from the date of death.

After paying all the individual bequests and settling expenses, the balance of the income of the estate will belong to the ultimate beneficiary (residuary legatee) — so called because they receive the residue of the estate. The residuary legatee is taxed on the amounts of income he receives from the executors in each tax year.

It is always a good idea to obtain clearance from the Tax Office that no further tax is payable before finally completing the administration and distribution of the estate.

Summary

- Make a will.
- Make maximum use of reliefs and exemptions.
- Consider the benefits of a deed of variation.

22

Estimating Your Tax Liability — Key Facts — 1996–97 and 1995–96

Personal taxation

Table 9 *Income tax rates*

Taxable income (£s)		Rate (%)	Cumulative tax (£s)	
1996–97	1995–96		1996–97	1995–96
1–3900	1–3200	20	780	640
3901–25,500	—	24	5964	—
—	3201–24,300	25	—	5915
over 25,500	over 24,300	40		

Notes: Tax is deducted at source at the rate of 20 per cent (25 per cent 1995–96) on savings income, otherwise it is at basic rate.
Tax credit on dividends at the lower rate of 20 per cent.
20 per cent rate not applicable to trusts.
Additional rate for discretionary trusts 10 per cent (10 per cent 1995–96)

Table 10 *Personal allowances*

	1996–97 £	1995–96 £
Personal	3765	3525
*Married couple's	1790	1720
*Additional relief for children	1790	1720
*Widow's bereavement	1790	1720
Blind person's	1250	1200
Age allowance 65–74:		
personal	4910	4630
*married couple's	3115	2995
income limit for relief	15,200	14,600

Age allowance 75 and over:

personal	5090	4800
*married couple's	3155	3035
income limit for full relief	15,200	14,600

* Restricted to 15 per cent for 1996–97 (15 per cent 1995–96)

Note: See Chapter 4 for additional explanation.

Personal reliefs

Interest relief on main residence:

- maximum loan £30,000;
- relief at the rate of 15 per cent (15 per cent 1995–96);
- new mortgages from 1 August 1988 relief restricted to £30,000 per property irrespective of number of borrowers.

Loss of office:

- £30,000 exempt — subject to special retirement rules.

Maintenance to ex-spouse (unless obligation existed on 15 March 1988):

- relief on maximum of £1790 per annum (£1720 1995–96).

Relief restricted to 15 per cent (15 per cent 1995–96)

Life assurance relief (pre 14 March 1984 policies):

- 12.5 per cent.

Vocational training:

- full relief for courses leading to certain qualifications.

'Rent a room' relief:

- rent received on furnished accommodation in an individual's residence tax-free £3250 (£3250 1995–96).

Payroll deduction:

- maximum gift to charity £1200 per annum (£900 1995–96).

Gift aid — minimum gift:

- from 16 March 1993 — £250

Personal incidental expenses paid by employer

- exemption for miscellaneous expenses on overnight stays away from home on business (eg newspapers, phone).
- Up to £5 per night in the UK or £10 per night abroad.

Benefits in kind

For all employees

Table 11 *Vans*

	Under 4 years old 1996–97 & 1995–96 £	4 years old and over 1996–97 & 1995–96 £
up to 3.5 tonnes	500†	350†
over 3.5 tonnes	nil	nil

†Per van.

For directors, and employees earning £8500 per annum or more including expense payments and benefits.

Mobile telephones: Scale charge of £200 per annum per telephone. (£200 1995–96)
No benefit if employee pays for all private calls.

Cars (1996–97 and 1995–96)

- 35 per cent of the list price when first registered and 35 per cent of the list price of any accessories (excluding accessories specifically designed for the disabled — from 1995–96)
- maximum price of car and accessories £80,000
- price reduced by some employee capital contributions
- benefit reduced by one third for 2500-17,999 business miles and two thirds for over 17,999 business miles
- resulting benefit further reduced by one third if car 4 years old and over and by private use contributions
- special rules apply for some cars over 15 years old
- where an employee is offered a cash alternative to the use of a company car he will, with effect from 1995–96, be assessed to income tax on the alternative he selects — car benefit or cash. This rule will also apply for the purpose of determining liability to Class 1A National Insurance Contributions.

Table 12 *Fuel*

	Diesel		Petrol	
	1996–97	**1995–96**	**1996–97**	**1995–96**
	£	**£**	**£**	**£**
up to 1400cc	640	605	710	670
1401–2000cc	640	605	890	850
over 2000cc	820	780	1320	1260

Note: No fuel benefit if employee pays for all private fuel or if fuel is only provided for business journeys.

Approved employee share schemes

See Chapter 10.

Profit-related pay schemes

See Chapter 10.

Retirement provision

Table 13 *Personal pension plans*

Age on 6 April	Maximum per cent of earnings†
35 or less	17.5
36–45	20.0
46–50	25.0
51–55	30.0
56–60	35.0
61–74	40.0

†May include up to 5 per cent for life cover.
Maximum earnings £82,200 (£78,600 1995–96).
Notes: Carry forward unused relief for 6 years.
Premiums paid may be treated as paid in previous year.

Table 14 *Existing retirement annuity plans*

Age on 6 April	Maximum per cent of earnings†
50 or less	17.5
51–55	20.0
56–60	22.5
61–74	27.5

†May include up to 5 per cent for life cover.

Capital gains tax

Individuals	charged at income tax rates
Discretionary trusts	34 per cent (35 per cent 1995–96)
For other trusts unless settlor or spouse can benefit	24 per cent (25 per cent 1995–96)

Table 15 *Capital gains tax*

	1996–97	1995–96
Annual exemptions (£s)		
individuals and personal representatives	6300	6000
trusts for disabled persons	6300	6000
other trusts (maximum)	3150	3000
Chattels exemption (maximum sale proceeds)	6000	6000
Retirement relief (£s) at 50 years (55 years: disposals before 28 November 1995)		
Exempt	1–250,000	1–250,000
50% relief	250,000–1,000,000	250,000–1,000,000

Note: Individual's trading losses available for offset against capital gains.

Inheritance tax

Table 16 *Inheritance tax*

Cumulative transfers (£s) from 6 April 1996

Transfers on death	**Rate per cent**
1–200,000	nil
over 200,000	40

Transfers within seven years of death *(number of years)*	**per cent of death rate charge**
0–3	100
3–4	80
4–5	60
5–6	40
6–7	20

Other chargeable lifetime transfers:
50 per cent death rate

Main exemptions and reliefs (£s)	
Annual gifts per donor	3000*
Small gifts per donee	250

Gifts on marriage	
parent	5000
grandparent or other direct lineal ancestor	2500
other	1000

Note: Business property relief 50% or 100%.
Agricultural property relief 50% or 100%.
* May be carried forward one year only.

Capital allowances

Table 17 *Capital allowances*

Year to 31 March	1997 Per cent	1996 Per cent
Plant and machinery writing down*†	25	25
Industrial, agricultural buildings and hotels writing down	4	4
Dredging and toll roads writing down	4	4
Enterprise zone buildings initial	100	100
writing down	25	25
Patent rights and know how writing down†	25	25
Scientific research	100	100

* Restricted for cars costing over £12,000.
† On reducing balance.

National insurance contributions

Table 18 *Class 1 employed — rates payable on all earnings*

From 6 April 1996

Earnings per week (£s)	Contracted in (%)		Contracted out (%)	
	employer	employee	employer	employee
61–109.99	3	*2/10	*3/Nil	*2/8.2
110–154.99	5	*2/10	*5/2	*2/8.2
155–209.99	7	*2/10	*7/4	*2/8.2
210–455.00	10.2	*2/10	*10.2/7.2	*2/8.2
over 455.00	10.2	£40.62	†10.2/7.2	£33.53

From 6 April 1995

Earnings per week (£s)	Contracted in (%)		Contracted out (%)	
	employer	employee	employer	employee
58–104.99	3	*2/10	3/nil	*2/8.2
105–149.99	5	*2/10	*5/2	*2/8.2
150–204.99	7	*2/10	*7/4	*2/8.2
205–440.00	10.2	*2/10	*10.2/7.2	*2/8.2
over 440.00	10.2	£39.36	†10.2/7.2	£32.48

* On first £61 (£58 1995–96).
† On first £61 (£58 1995–96) and on earnings in excess of £455 (£440 1995–96).
Notes: Employer's NIC of 10.2 per cent (10.2 per cent 1995–96) payable on income tax scale rates applicable to company cars and car fuel.
Employee's rate for married woman with valid election 3.85 per cent (3.85 per cent 1995–96) on all earnings up to £455 per week (£440 1995–96), if earnings exceed £60.99 per week (£57.99 1995–96).

Table 19 *Class 2 self-employed*

	1996–97	1995–96
Flat rate	£6.05 per week	£5.75 per week
Small earnings exception	£3430 per annum	£3260 per annum

Table 20 *Class 3 non-employed*

	1996–97	1995–96
Voluntary	£5.95 per week	£5.65 per week

Table 21 *Class 4 self-employed*

	1996–97	1995–96
Rate on profits	6%	7.3%
Annual lower limit	£6860	£6640
Annual upper limit	£23,660	£22,880
Maximum per annum	£1,008.00	£1,185.52

Note: No tax relief is allowed on Class 4 contributions (50 per cent relief 1995–96).

Value added tax

Standard rate 17.5 per cent

Fraction $^7/_{47}$ when applied to a VAT-inclusive figure gives the amount of VAT, for example,

$$£200 + \text{VAT at } 17.5\% \text{ of } £35 = £235$$
$$^7/_{47} \times £235 = £35$$

Fuel and power for domestic use 8 per cent. Fraction $^2/_{27}$

Registration threshold from 29 November 1995 £47,000 (£46,000 from 30 November 1994).

Deregistration threshold from 29 November 1995 £45,000 (£44,000 from 30 November 1994).

Maximum turnover for cash accounting scheme £350,000.

Maximum turnover for annual accounting £300,000.

Table 22 *VAT element of fuel benefit*

All scale rates should be used from the start of the next VAT accounting period beginning on or after 6 April. The quarterly rates are:

	Diesel (£s)		Petrol (£s)	
	1996–97	1995–96	1996–97	1995–96
up to 1400cc	23.82	22.48	26.36	24.87
1401–2000cc	23.82	22.48	33.06	31.57
over 2000cc	30.53	29.04	49.14	46.91

(Bad debt relief waiting period 6 months from date of supply)

	From 1 January 1995
Penalties for late registration†	
up to 9 months late	5%*
up to 18 months late	10%*
over 18 months late	15%*
late returns or payment	2–15%*
serious misdeclaration†	15%‡
civil fraud†	100%‡

† Mitigation available.
* Of the related tax.
‡ Of the tax underdeclared.

Normal due dates for payment of tax

Income tax	See Chapter 1
Corporation tax	9 months after accounts date
Advance corporation tax	14 days after period end
Capital gains tax	{ 31 January 1998 (1996–97) { 1 December 1996 (1995–96)

Inheritance tax

on death or transfer 1 October–5 April	6 months after end of month in which death/transfer occurs
on transfer 6 April–30 September	30 April after tax year
Value added tax	1 month after period end

Social security benefits

Table 23 *Weekly rates*

	Non taxable (£s)	
	1996–97	1995–96
Child benefit		
first child	10.80	10.40
each subsequent child	8.80	8.45
One parent benefit	6.30	6.30
Incapacity benefit		
long term	61.15	58.85
short term		
– lower rate	46.15	44.40
– higher rate	54.55	52.50
State maternity allowance		
– self employed/unemployed	47.35	45.55
– employed	54.55	52.50

Stamp duty

Table 24 *Rates of duty*

Shares*	0.5%
Land and buildings over £60,000	1%
Other chargeable transfers*	1%
Gifts and gilts	nil

* Under review

Appendix A
Indexation allowance
— Retail Prices Index

	1982	1983	1984	1985	1986	1987	1988	1989	1990	1991	1992	1993	1994	1995
January	—	82.6	86.8	91.2	96.2	100.0	103.3	111.0	119.5	130.2	135.6	137.9	141.3	146.0
February	—	83.0	87.2	91.9	96.6	100.4	103.7	111.8	120.2	130.9	136.3	138.8	142.1	146.9
March	79.4	83.1	87.5	92.8	96.7	100.6	104.1	112.3	121.4	131.4	136.7	139.3	142.5	147.5
April	81.0	84.3	88.6	94.8	97.7	101.8	105.8	114.3	125.1	133.1	138.8	140.6	144.2	149.0
May	81.6	84.6	89.0	95.2	97.8	101.9	106.2	115.0	126.2	133.5	139.3	141.1	144.7	149.6
June	81.9	84.8	89.2	95.4	97.8	101.9	106.6	115.4	126.7	134.1	139.3	141.0	144.7	149.8
July	81.9	85.3	89.1	95.2	97.5	101.8	106.7	115.5	126.8	133.8	138.8	140.7	144.0	149.1
August	81.9	85.7	89.9	95.5	97.8	102.1	107.9	115.8	128.1	134.1	138.9	141.3	144.7	149.9
September	81.9	86.1	90.1	95.4	98.3	102.4	108.4	116.6	129.3	134.6	139.4	141.9	145.0	150.6
October	82.3	86.4	90.7	95.6	98.5	102.9	109.5	117.5	130.3	135.1	139.9	141.8	145.2	149.8
November	82.7	86.7	91.0	95.9	99.3	103.4	110.0	118.5	130.0	135.6	139.7	141.6	145.3	149.8
December	82.5	86.9	90.9	96.0	99.6	103.3	110.3	118.8	129.9	135.7	139.2	141.9	146.0	150.7

Allowance = Acquisition cost/31 March 1982 market value x $\dfrac{RD - RI}{RI}$

RD = Retail prices index for month in which disposal occurred.

RI = Retail prices index for either March 1982 or month in which acquisition occurred, whichever is the later.

Appendix B
The Taxpayer's Charter*

You are entitled to expect the Inland Revenue

To be fair

- by settling your tax affairs impartially;
- by expecting you to pay only what is due under the law;
- by treating everyone with equal fairness.

To help you

- to get your tax affairs right;
- to understand your rights and obligations;
- by providing clear leaflets and forms;
- by giving you information and assistance at our enquiry offices;
- by being courteous at all times.

To provide an efficient service

- by settling your tax affairs promptly and accurately;
- by keeping your private affairs strictly confidential;
- by using the information you give us only as allowed by the law;
- by keeping our costs down.

To be accountable for what we do

- by setting standards for ourselves and publishing how well we live up to them.

---

* Crown copyright is reproduced with the permission of the Controller of HMSO.

If you are not satisfied

- we will tell you exactly how to complain;
- you can ask for your tax affairs to be looked at again;
- you can appeal to an independent tribunal;
- your MP can refer your complaint to the Ombudsman.

In return, we need you

- to be honest;
- to give us accurate information;
- to pay your tax on time.

Appendix C
The Contributor's Charter*

A message from the Chief Executive

Since we published our Charter for Contributors in August 1991 we have worked hard to improve our service. We are therefore pleased to publish a new Contributor's Charter which reflects improvements we have made to our service.

For example, early research showed that most customers want to conduct as much of their business as possible by telephone, so we installed more direct telephone lines in our offices.

National insurance is collected direct from you if you are self-employed, or if you make voluntary contributions. If you are employed it is deducted from your pay by your employer.

Your national insurance contribution, **unlike income tax,** does affect entitlement to benefit for you and your family.

This new Contributor's Charter:

- Sets out the new and improved standards of service you can expect.
- Tells you what we do.
- Tells you how to get more help and information.

What you can expect from us:

- Carry out checks on national insurance records to ensure they are as complete, accurate and up-to-date as possible.
- If there are any problems with your national insurance, we will tell you what we are doing, or you can do, to put things right.
- Whether on the phone or in letters, our staff will tell you their name and be courteous and helpful.

We will also:

- Deal with your national insurance affairs fairly and impartially.
- Treat any information you give us in confidence.

Faith Boardman
Chief Executive

---

* The version of The Contributor's Charter being reproduced here is the April 1995 issue. It is reproduced by kind permission of the Contributions Agency.

Our key standards
Correspondence

If you contact us and we need to reply in writing we will do so within 10 working days of receiving your enquiry.

If we cannot answer all of your questions within that time, we will let you know:

- why not *and*
- when you can expect a full reply.

Our letters will be clear and easy to understand.

If you phone us

If you phone us, we will answer your query immediately, if we can. If this is not possible, we will:

- tell you why *and*
- let you know when you can expect a full reply.

Visiting our offices

We usually share premises with the Benefits Agency and the receptionist you see works for them.

Benefits Agency staff can answer straightforward questions about national insurance.

If you call at the office you can expect:

- The staff you see to wear name badges.
- The Benefits Agency receptionist to see you within 10 minutes. At very busy times this may not always be possible. But, even so, you should not wait more than 30 minutes.
- A private interview if you ask for one.

If your query is complex, a member of the Contributions Agency staff will either:

- come to see you *or*
- arrange an appointment within two weeks of your visit.

Visiting you

If you need information from us but have a disability which prevents you coming to our office, please phone or write explaining the problem and what you need from us. We will make the necessary arrangements to visit you.
We will:

- respond within one week of receiving your request *and*
- visit within the following two weeks.

We are required to visit employers and the self-employed to confirm they are dealing with their national insurance properly. If we visit you and you are self-employed, we will:

- Normally tell you in advance, agree a convenient time and let you know the name of the person calling.
- Tell you in advance what documents we will need to see, to keep the time spent on your premises to a minimum.
- Help you with any national insurance problems you may have.
- Leave a contact name in case you have any queries after the visit.

If you prefer, we can usually offer to see you at one of our offices.

All our visiting staff carry identification and will show it to you when they arrive.

National Insurance details

- We aim to give national insurance details to benefit offices within 24 hours to enable payments to be made on time.
- If you have a claim to benefit refused because the information we hold is wrong, you can give the Employment Service or Benefits Agency other evidence of the national insurance you have paid, eg form P60 or wage slips.
- When you start or terminate a private pension, we receive details from the insurance company. We aim to update our records within 24 working days.

Advice and information
How to contact us

You can phone or write to any of our offices for advice about:

- National insurance contributions.
- Statutory Sick Pay.
- Statutory Maternity Pay.
- The effect your personal pension arrangements have on national insurance rates.

The address and phone numbers of our offices can be found in the phone directory under either:

- 'Contributions Agency' or
- 'Social Security, Department of'.

Helplines

For advice about other matters, we have special helplines. These are open on Monday to Thursday from 8.30am to 4.30pm and 8.30am to 4.00pm on Fridays.

At other times you can leave a message on an answerphone. Messages will be dealt with at the start of the next working day.

All calls to our helplines are charged at BT's local rate.

Contracted-out and personal pensions Helpline

For general enquiries about contracting-out and personal pensions. Telephone **06451 50150.**

Direct Debit Helpline

For the self-employed and those making voluntary payments who want to know more about direct debit and quarterly billing, or who have queries about their payments. Telephone **06451 54451.**

Overseas Contributions Helpline

For advice for people working abroad about paying national insurance contributions. Telephone **06451 54811.**

Benefits Agency Freeline

For free and confidential general information about Social Security benefits.

Available on weekdays between 8.30am and 4.30pm, with some regional variations.
Telephone **0800 666 555**, calls are free.

Pay As You Earn (PAYE)

If you have an enquiry about PAYE, contact your nearest tax enquiry centre.

The address and phone number can be found in the telephone directory under Inland Revenue.

If your first language is not English

If you wish to deal with us in Welsh please let us know and we will arrange for this to be done.

If English or Welsh is not your first language, please let us know. We can provide an interpreter or make other suitable arrangements.

Leaflets

We publish a range of information leaflets. Our leaflet CA48 'Useful information and contacts for contributors' gives the full list.

You can get copies of our leaflets from any Contributions Agency or Social Security office.

If you want five or more copies of a leaflet, please write, or send a fax, to:

HMSO
Oldham Broadway Business Park
Broadgate
Chadderton
Oldham
OL9 0JA
Fax number 0161 683 2395

You can get general information about contributory social security benefits in leaflet FB2 'Which Benefit', available from Social Security offices or by phoning the Benefits Agency Freeline, see above.

Over the next two years, we will review all our leaflets to make sure they give you all the information you need in a clear and simple way.

We welcome any comments you have. Please write to the Corporate Customer Services Manager, see page 160.

What to do if things go wrong

Despite our best efforts, we know we do not always get everything right first time.

Problems and errors are frequently put right more quickly by the person or office you have been dealing with.

All of our staff will be happy to deal with any comments you may have, or you may prefer to deal with one of our managers.

If you are not satisfied with the service you have received, please get in touch with the Contributions Agency staff member or Manager of the office you deal with.

You can write, phone, send a fax, come to the office or return the tear-off slip in the complaints leaflet, CA62, to explain the problem.

The Contributions Manager will:

- Investigate your complaint impartially and fairly, giving a full or informed interim reply within five working days.
- Apologise and give an explanation where we have given poor service.
- Put right any mistakes.

If you are still not satisfied, you can write to our Chief Executive:

Room C1837
Contributions Agency
DSS Longbenton
Newcastle Upon Tyne
NE98 1YX

The Chief Executive will:

- Investigate your complaint.
- Reply within 10 working days of receiving your complaint.

If a full response is not possible in that time you will be told when you can expect a reply.

What to do if you are still not happy

To ensure there is an independent avenue of complaint against the Agency, there will be, from 1 June 1995, an Independent Adjudicator.

The Adjudicator also acts as an impartial referee for the Inland Revenue and Customs and Excise.

Where our Chief Executive has not been able to settle your complaint, or you do not think you have been treated fairly, you can ask the Adjudicator, Elizabeth Filkin, to consider the matter and recommend appropriate action.

Please note: the arrangement we have with the Adjudicator is that she will only consider cases which have been examined by our Chief Executive first.

The Adjudicator will also normally only look at a complaint or problem if the request is made no more than six months after our Chief Executive has provided an answer with which you are not satisfied.

Further information about the way the Adjudicator can help you can be found in our complaints leaflet, CA62, or from the:

Adjudicator's Office
3rd floor
Haymarket House
28 Haymarket
London
SW1Y 4SP
Tel: 0171 930 2292

You can also seek independent help, see page 157.

Special payments

We make every effort to deal with your national insurance affairs quickly and properly. Occasionally, however, we make mistakes and sometimes take longer than necessary to handle matters.

If we do, there are certain circumstances when we can consider making a special payment.

We may be able to do so if you have suffered actual financial loss because we made an error in dealing with your case or because we gave you wrong information.

We can also consider a special payment if, because of an error by us, your contribution refund has been unacceptably delayed:

- the delay must be more than 12 months *and*
- the amount we owe you must be at least £50.

If you think any of these circumstances applies to you please get in touch with the Contributions Manager of the office you have been dealing with, who will advise you what to do next.

Whilst there is no legal right to a special payment, we will consider each case individually. However, payment in one case does not set a precedent for other similar cases.

If you want to challenge a decision

If you are not satisfied with a decision we have given about your national insurance or the amount you have to pay, you have a legal right to challenge that decision.

Our staff will explain how you can do this.

Independent advice

If you would like independent advice, you can contact:

- The Citizen's Advice Bureau.
- A professional advisor, eg accountant or solicitor.
  Please note: that we will only meet the costs for this in very exceptional circumstances
- A trade association or trade union.
- Your Member of Parliament.

Members of Parliament can ask the Parliamentary Commissioner for Administration, the Ombudsman, to investigate on your behalf. You can find out more about the Ombudsman by contacting:

**Office of the Parliamentary Commissioner for
    Administration
Church House
Great Smith Street
London
SW1P 3BW
Tel: 0171 276 2130 or 3000**

Letting you know how we perform

We want to give the best possible service. At the moment 80 per cent of customers, surveyed independently, are satisfied with our service. We aim to steadily improve on this.

During 1994/95 we will develop ways of comparing the performance of different parts of the Agency against key Charter commitments and publish details in our 1995/96 Business Plan.

We will publish our performance results:

- In our Annual Reports and Business Plans, see page 159 for details of how to obtain copies.
- By displaying them in all our offices.

What you can do

Your national insurance number

Employers need to deduct tax and national insurance as soon as they start paying you.

If they do not have your national insurance number they usually create a temporary one. This will begin TN. You should give your employer your proper national insurance number as soon as possible.

If you have forgotten your national insurance number or do not yet have one, contact the nearest Contributions Agency or Social Security office. They can advise you.

Protecting confidentiality

It is very important that your employer has your correct national insurance number. This number is unique to you and it is in your best interest to ensure it does not get into the wrong hands. If you have any doubts about giving it to someone please contact your local Contributions Agency office.

For example, if anyone phones unexpectedly to say you may be entitled to a refund of national insurance contributions and asks you for personal details, you should ask for their phone number *without giving any details*. Ask your local Contributions Agency office to confirm the caller works for us.

Helping us keep accurate personal details

Write and tell your local Contributions Agency office if you change your name or address so we can continue to record the contributions on your national insurance account quickly and accurately.

Protecting your state pension

If you are below retirement age but have no earnings on which national insurance can be charged, you can make voluntary contributions to protect your state pension.

Our leaflet 'National Insurance – Voluntary Contributions', CA08, gives more information.

If you want information about the contributions you have paid

You can ask for a statement showing your contributions record by writing to:

Contributions Queries
DSS Longbenton
Newcastle upon Tyne
NE98 1YX

Please quote your national insurance number.

Help us to improve our service

You can help us to improve the service we give you by:

- Always quoting your national insurance number when you phone or write to us.
- Giving us all the facts and documents we ask for.
- Giving us your full name and a phone number or fax number in case we need further information.
- Writing to the Corporate Customer Services Manager if you have any ideas on what we can do to improve the service we offer. See page 160 for details.

Further information

For copies of the Contributions Agency's:

- Business Plan.
- Annual Report.

- Standards and Performance.
- Customer Charters.

Contact:

Vic Hillier
Corporate Customer Services Manager
Contributions Agency
Room 76J
DSS Longbenton
Newcastle Upon Tyne
NE98 1YX
Tel: 0191 22 55134

Appendix D
Residence, Ordinary Residence and Domicile

Unfortunately, the tax legislation does not define the terms residence and ordinary residence and their meanings are largely based on the interpretations of the Courts which in many cases go back to the 1920s. While the decisions are helpful, they were very much dependent upon their own particular circumstances. However, the Inland Revenue have evolved a set of rules based on these Court Decisions which are generally accepted.

Residence

Residence status is considered by reference to an income tax year and is therefore reviewed each year. For most people, their status does not change but for a few it is possible to be regarded as resident one year but not the next and vice versa. Residence requires physical presence in the UK for at least part of the year. If an individual is present, and for more than 183 days, then the Inland Revenue will regard him as resident for that year. Conversely, if someone is not present for a whole year, then they would be regarded as not resident. The concept of resident also applies in other countries and so it is possible to be resident in the UK and also resident in another country. There are usually rules and agreements between countries to avoid any such problems.

Ordinary residence

Ordinary residence suggests a degree of permanence in the UK and more than just physical presence. If an individual comes to the UK and intends to remain here, then they would be regarded as ordinarily resident from the day of arrival. However, if they are only visiting then they could be resident, by being here for more than 183 days, but not ordinarily resident as they normally live abroad. Habitual visits to the UK, where such visits are for more than 91 days per year on average over a four-year period, will lead the Inland Revenue to regard the visitor as ordinarily resident from the beginning of the fifth tax year. Similarly, if someone leaves the UK then, to be regarded as not ordinarily resident, they have to show they have severed their ties with the UK. This is often difficult and may require the sale of the family home and disposal of the furniture. It is also the practice of the Inland Revenue to defer giving a final ruling on residence status until three years after departure to live abroad. They would consider visits to the UK and, after giving a final ruling, make any adjustments to a UK tax bill. The only exception is for individuals who go to work overseas for a complete income-tax year. By concession, these would be regarded as non-resident and not ordinarily resident from the day following the date they leave.

Domicile

Domicile is a difficult concept. Broadly, an individual's domicile is the country he regards as his natural home. For most people, their domicile is their country of birth and is known as Domicile of Origin. It is possible to change a domicile of origin by going to another country to live there permanently. This is a Domicile of Choice, but it is necessary to show that there is no intention to return to the original country. One way of showing intent to stay in the new country that has been used by the famous is to buy a burial plot in that country. If the domicile of origin were the UK and remained so at death then a worldwide liability to UK inheritance tax exists wherever the individual was living at the time.

Appendix E
Intestacy Rules — England and Wales

The following are the main provisions of the intestacy rules as at 1 December 1993.

Surviving Relative(s)	Person(s) Entitled to the Estate		Person(s) Entitled to Grant of Letters of Administration
Spouse only	Spouse absolutely		Surviving spouse
Spouse and children	Spouse takes:	Personal chattels £125,000 Life interest in half of residue	Surviving spouse and one other person
	Children take:	Life interest in other half of residue until attaining 18 when they take an absolute interest in equal share *per stirpes**	
Spouse and parents	Spouse takes:	Personal chattels £200,000 Half of residue	Surviving spouse
	Parents take:	Half of residue shared equally between them	
Spouse and brothers and/or sisters and/or children of such who predeceased the intestate	Spouse takes:	Personal chattels £200,000 Half of residue	Surviving spouse and one other person
	Brothers and sisters/and/or children take:	Half of residue on attaining 18 in equal shares *per stirpes**	
Children	Children take:	Entire estate at age 18 in equal shares *per stirpes**	Children

Parents	Parents take the entire estate equally	Parents
Brothers/and/or sisters and/or children of such who predeceased the intestate	Brothers and sisters (or their children) take the entire estate equally (at age 18) *per stirpes**	Brother or sister or children and one other person
Half brothers and/or sisters and/or children of such who predeceased the intestate	Half brothers and sisters (or their children) take the entire estate equally (at age 18) *per stirpes**	Half brother or sister or children and one other person
Grandparents	Grandparents in equal shares	Grandparent
Uncles and/or aunts and/or children of such who have predeceased the intestate	Uncles and aunts and/or children at age 18 in equal shares *per stirpes**	Uncle, aunt or cousins and one other person
Half uncles and/or aunts and/or children of such who have predeceased the intestate	Half uncles and/or aunts and/or children at age 18 in equal shares *per stirpes**	Half uncle, aunt or children and one other person
No relative as above	The Crown	The Crown

Note: Common law husbands or wives derive no benefit under the intestacy rules.
**Per stirpes* is Latin and literally means 'by the stem'. Where their deceased parent would have benefited but for their early death then the children of the parent can take the share in their stead.

Appendix F
Intestacy Rules — Scotland

Where a Scottish domiciled person dies intestate, certain rules come into operation which are intended to make provision for the surviving spouse and any issue of the deceased — these are known respectively as Prior Rights and Legal Rights. (Legal Rights also apply where the deceased person has left a valid will. The Rights cannot be extinguished by the will).

Prior Rights

The aim of Prior Rights (which take precedence over Legal Rights) is to ensure, where possible, that the widow/widower is left with a furnished house and a reasonable amount of money. These rights can only be claimed by a surviving spouse.

Divorced spouses have no claim on the deceased's property unless they benefit under a will.

Where a couple, not married to one another, have been cohabiting, the surviving partner may attempt to establish a claim by obtaining a Declarator of Marriage from the Court of Session (this may prove difficult to achieve). If successful, this would mean that the partner could then be treated as a spouse.

The following assets are affected by Prior Rights:

- The dwelling house.
- The furniture.
- Money.

The dwelling house

The surviving spouse is entitled to ownership of the house in which he/she resided prior to the death of the other spouse and which was owned by the deceased. In certain circumstances the spouse must take the value of the house in money instead of the property itself. This will usually be where the house forms part of a larger property, eg farm and farmhouse. If the deceased owned more than one house at the date of death, the spouse has the choice, provided he/she lived in both regularly.

The value of the house must not exceed £110,000. If it is worth more than this, the spouse is entitled to £110,000 in money in lieu of the house.

The furniture

The surviving spouse is entitled to all the furnishings in a house up to the value of £20,000. The furniture, eg tables, chairs, beds, cooker, fridge, etc must have been owned by the deceased outright at the date of death and not held simply under a hire-purchase or credit agreement.

Personal items such as jewellery do not fall into this category. The right to the furniture is separate from the right to the house. Therefore, if the surviving spouse takes money instead of the property, this will not affect his/her right to furnishings.

Money

The surviving spouse is also entitled to a sum of money in addition to any money he/she received in lieu of the dwelling house. Where the deceased is survived only by a spouse and no children, the entitlement is £50,000. If there are surviving children, the entitlement is limited to £30,000.

Legal Rights

These are the rights that may be claimed by a surviving spouse and/or children, and are claimed out of the moveable part of the estate (property which can be moved — not land and houses). The amount granted under this right is dependent upon where the deceased is survived by only a spouse, or only children, or both.

- If the spouse alone survives, his/her Legal Rights will amount to one half of the remainder of the moveable property after deduction of the debts, funeral expenses, a proportion of the expenses of administration and Prior Rights of money and furniture.
- If only children survive, they will be entitled to one half of the estate divided equally between them. If the deceased parent has already given a child a substantial gift during his/her lifetime, its value at that time may be offset against that child's entitlement to Legal Rights.

- If both the spouse and children survive, then the moveable estate, less Prior Rights so far as taken from the moveable estate, is divided into equal parts. One third goes to the widow/widower, one third is divided between the children and the remaining third is divided as part of the free estate (see below).

Note: If a testator dies leaving a mortgaged house where the mortgage is secured by an insurance policy, the value of the policy has to be apportioned between the heritable and moveable estates for the purpose of calculating the Legal Rights entitlement.

Division of Free Estate

The remainder of the property (the free estate) is divided in the following manner.

Everything is taken by:

- Issue, but if none:
- Parents and brothers or sisters (half to parents, half to brothers and sisters).

If there are no parents, the brothers and sisters take the balance and if there are no brothers and sisters, then the parents take the balance and if there are no brothers and sisters or parents:

- The surviving spouse, but if none;
- Uncles and aunts or their descendants, but if none;
- Grandparents, but if none;
- Brothers and sisters of grandparents or their descendants, but if none;
- Remoter ancestors of the intestate, generation by generation successively, but if none;
- The Crown (if no relations can be found the Crown takes the estate as ultimate heir).

Notes

- In Scottish law, 'issue' is defined as children (including illegitimate and adopted children), grandchildren and so on but not step-children (this is the same situation as in England and Wales and in Northern Ireland).
- In applying the rules relating to Prior Rights, Legal Rights and the division of the free estate, it should be noted that issue are entitled by representation to take the share of a parent who has died.

Appendix G
Intestacy Rules — Northern Ireland

Where the intestate leaves:

1. **Surviving spouse but no issue and no parents or brothers or sisters or half brothers or half sisters:**
Surviving spouse takes the whole estate.

2. **Surviving spouse and issue:**

(A) Surviving spouse takes:
- £125,000 (or whole estate, if less); *and*
- Personal chattels; *and*
- Half of the remaining estate where one child survives the intestate, or one-third if more than one child survives the intestate. However, if a child of the intestate predeceases him, leaving issue of his own, the surviving spouse's share of the estate is calculated as if the deceased child has survived the intestate.

(B) Issue take equal shares between them, one-half of the remaining estate (if one child or one deceased child with surviving issue) or two-thirds of the remaining estate (if more than one child and/or deceased child with surviving issue).

3. **Surviving spouse and no issue but parents or brothers or sisters or half brothers or half sisters:**

(A) Surviving spouse takes:
- £200,000 (or whole estate, if less); *and*
- Personal chattels; *and*
- One-half ("the first half") of the remaining estate.

(B) The surviving parents take the second half of the remaining estate

(C) If no parents are alive, the brothers and sisters and half brothers and half sisters take the second half of the remaining estate in equal shares.

4. Issue but no surviving spouse:

The issue take the whole estate in equal shares.

5. No surviving spouse or issue:

The whole estate passes to the following in order of priority:
- Parents, failing whom
- Brothers and sisters and half brothers and half sisters (who are all treated equally), failing whom
- Next of kin, failing whom
- The Crown.

Note: The share of a deceased's estate taken by the surviving spouse is an absolute interest and not just a life interest.

Appendix H
The Introduction of Self-Assessment and the Adoption of the Current Year Basis of Assessment for Schedule D

Introduction

In the next two years the UK tax system faces radical changes to the way in which tax returns are completed and the means by which tax on certain types of income is assessed and paid. The changes have been referred to as a move to 'Self-assessment' and a change to the 'Current Year' basis.

The change to 'self-assessment' involves the completion of a new style tax return for 1996–97 which, at the taxpayer's option, will enable the taxpayer to 'self-assess' or calculate his or her own tax liability for the tax year. To assist with this, the Inland Revenue are moving certain taxpayer's records so that, in future, all taxpayers will only deal with the tax district under one tax reference.

The change to the 'current year' basis principally affects self-employed taxpayers from 1997–98 onwards. Under existing rules traders have been taxed on their business profits under what is known as the 'preceding year' basis. Profits of an accounting period ending in one tax year form the basis of assessment for the next tax year. For example, the accounts period to 30 June 1992 ended in the tax year 1992–93, but would be used as a basis for tax demands raised for 1993–94. The new current year system will tax the profits of the business in the same tax year as that in which the accounts period ends. For example, the accounts period to 30 June 1998 ends in the tax year 1998–99 and profits of that period will be taxed in 1998–99.

The moves to self-assessment and current year basis will not affect the majority of taxpayers — those who are employees and whose affairs are dealt with under the PAYE system. That will continue, largely unchanged. However, to ensure that taxpayers have the necessary information about their employment to include on a tax form, the government has introduced rules requiring employers to provide details to employees about their income and benefits in kind. The Inland Revenue have also given guidance on the nature of records that taxpayers should maintain and have available in the event of enquiries into accounts and returns.

On the other hand, directors of companies, those with untaxed income, those liable to the higher rate of tax on part of their income and the self-employed will be affected by the changes. The following paragraphs are only a brief outline of the changes, a detailed consideration of the new rules is outside the scope of this book.

Self-assessment

The first year of self-assessment is the tax year 1996–97. New tax returns devised by the Inland Revenue are to be issued to taxpayers in April 1997 and subsequent years.

The tax form embodies the move to self-assessment as it is not only a summary of income and gains and a claim for personal tax allowances, but also includes an option for the taxpayer to calculate the balance of outstanding tax payable for the year. The detail underlying the figures on the form is included on a number of schedules also to be submitted to the Inland Revenue.

If a taxpayer would prefer the Inland Revenue to calculate and assess the tax outstanding, the completed tax form must be submitted to the Tax Office by 30 September following the end of the tax year. A tax assessment will be raised and any outstanding tax will be payable by 31 January after the end of the tax year.

The taxpayer who self-assesses will be able to submit the form up to 31 January in the year after the tax year, and any balance of tax will also be payable on or before that date.

Self-employed taxpayers

From 6 April 1994 any new unincorporated business will be taxed under the current year basis rules whilst existing businesses will be subject to transitional rules for 1996–97 before coming completely into line with the new system for 1997–98.

In advance of the new system coming fully into force the main considerations for the self-employed taxpayer concern the date to which they draw up their accounts and the way in which profits will fall out of charge to tax in the transitional period. Specific professional advice should be sought as soon as possible as the Inland Revenue have introduced certain measures to counteract tax avoidance where there is not a compelling and overriding commercial reason to support the action taken.

Tax payments

Under self-assessment and the current year basis, tax payments will be due on three dates:

- 31 January in the tax year;
- 31 July after the end of the tax year (the same amount as the January payment);
  — interim payments both initially estimated on the basis of the payments made in the year before; and
- 31 January in the year following the tax year for which the payment is due. This is the balance payment following the calculation of the final liability on the tax form but it also includes any tax payable on capital gains.

In the move to self-assessment, payment dates will be as follows:

1 December 1996	1995/96	Capital Gains Tax
		Higher Rate Tax
When assessed	1995/96	Schedule E
31 January 1997	1996/97	First interim payment on account
31 July 1997	1996/97	Second interim payment on account
31 January 1998	1996/97	Balance of income tax
	1996/97	Capital gains tax
	1997/98	First interim payment on account
31 July 1988	1997/98	Second interim payment on account

The above payment dates do not just apply to self-employed taxpayers.

Penalties and interest

Accompanying the system of self-assessment is a new regime of penalties, interest and surcharges intended to ensure compliance with the new rules. In most cases the financial impositions are fixed and automatic and can only be mitigated if a 'reasonable excuse' can be proved. The view of the Inland Revenue as to what constitutes a reasonable excuse is limited.

Index